Trade Secrets

How to Protect Your Ideas and Assets

Trade Secrets

How to Protect Your Ideas and Assets

By James Pooley

Illustrations by
James E. Hummell

Osborne/McGraw-Hill
Berkeley, California

Published by
Osborne/McGraw-Hill
630 Bancroft Way
Berkeley, California 94710
USA

For information on other Osborne books, translations and distributors outside of the U.S.A., please write Osborne/McGraw-Hill at the above address.

TRADE SECRETS: HOW TO PROTECT YOUR IDEAS AND ASSETS

ISBN 0-931988-72-1

1 2 3 4 5 6 7 8 9 0 HCHC 8 9 0 9 8 7 6 5 4 3 2

A legal review of this book was performed by Roger Borovoy, J.D.

Jacket design by Timothy Sullivan.

For Fran, Jeff, and Chris

Contents

Acknowledgments

The task of writing this book has not been mine alone. I am grateful for assistance from Martin Fliesler, a San Francisco patent attorney who provided counsel in his area of expertise. Excellent comments and suggestions also came from Roger Borovoy, general counsel for Intel Corporation, and my good friend Paul Rice, a local business lawyer. Thanks also go to Joann Harper and Betty Wilson, who have assisted in the myriad administrative details. Denise Penrose, my editor, has done a wonderful job of making the text a thing of beauty. Most of the credit, however, must be shared by Susan Wong, a tireless and enthusiastic typist and indexer, and my wife Fran, who gave me the support that made this possible.

Introduction

Ideas mean money in today's world, since industry relies on technology to improve productivity. Your ability to do well or even survive in the resulting highly competitive climate will largely depend on your success in acquiring, protecting, and exploiting a piece of that technology.

Your competitive edge also depends on developing and protecting your business information, such as marketing studies, customer lists, and the like. At the same time, these increasingly valuable ideas and "intellectual property" lie in the hands of a fairly mobile, independent, and decreasingly loyal work force. The order of the day is the "split-off start-up," which means disgruntled or opportunistic employees (depending on your bias) leave to compete directly with their former employers.

Whether an employer or an employee, you must be armed with the knowledge of how to use and guard your ideas, and how to thrive in the midst of this tumult. That is what trade secrets are all about and why reading this book should be important to you.

A central theme underlying this effort postulates that intellectual property, technology, or "proprietary information" is an *asset*. In many ways this information resembles the raw materials used to make products, a company's capital equipment, or plant, or inventory on the shelf. It may or may not cost a lot to acquire (in fact, it may be discovered by accident), but proprietary information certainly is valuable and depreciates over time if not put to productive use.

You can use this material to produce valuable goods or services, or turn it into cash by selling it to others to commercialize. And truer of intellectual property than of any other asset, it can easily be lost or stolen.

Among all the assets a business owns, its proprietary information may well be the most important. It can ameliorate the effect of today's soaring costs for labor, energy, and raw materials on productivity and profitability. Now, more than at any time in our history, we must learn to cultivate and control our intellectual property.

At the same time, we must adjust to one frustrating aspect of technology that distinguishes it from other assets: it is often volatile and short-lived. This volatility results from the increasing pace of technological change, which often obsoletes perfectly good inventions before they can be brought to the marketplace. This circumstance probably will not improve. As most observers agree, technological advances are proceeding at an exponential pace. However, that does not mean that you should simply throw up your hands and forget about the whole mess. It does require you to be jealously protective of your proprietary information, and to fervently work to capitalize on it as soon as possible.

Paradoxically, as technology becomes a more important and volatile asset, it becomes more expensive to produce. Computer software typifies this problem. While hardware engineering and production time is relatively short, preparing several hundred thousand lines of code is time-consuming and enormously expensive. Although scientists are developing computer systems that will create programs, until such artificial intelligence becomes available, software development will require this labor-intensive effort. Because it can be so easily copied, software exemplifies an extremely expensive type of intellectual property which requires careful, even fanatical, protection while its development costs are recouped through sales.

Also consider that the technological revolution has vastly increased the ease of communication and trade across state and national boundaries. One effect of this development is keener competition. Given relatively equivalent access to the raw materials of commerce, the success of most businesses will depend on their abilities to protect and exploit both their technology and other proprietary data. Unlike the days when a company's competitive advantage derived from its proximity to a railroad or a mine, today a business is primarily distinguished from others by that proprietary data.

Just as more businesses enjoy interstate and international trade, employees have also picked up their roots. Rising affluence and the acquisition of more generally applicable skills have made it easier for employees to move from place to place, and from job to job. In many fields, employees now expect and want to move regularly, in contrast to earlier times when a successful career meant staying in one place. Now, we find an increasingly critical asset is placed in less controllable, less loyal hands. The need for special measures to protect that asset is apparent.

Technology has also made it easier for an employee to leave and compete directly with his former employer. Today small businesses are often created solely to trade on a specific, new technological advantage that larger companies, with their slower, more cumbersome organizations, cannot exploit. Extensive capital is often less of a problem. If you require and deserve it, financing is usually easy to get, apart from traditional bank funding. And the rapid pace of change and simpler, more effective interstate communication have facilitated market penetration by even the smallest new enterprises. These developments present fabulous new opportunities for employees wanting to strike out on their own, and they also present serious, difficult challenges to the established employer.

This is not a book about industrial espionage per se. It does describe how to avoid simple carelessness, which causes significant trade secret losses. Too many businesses operate like banks which not only leave the doors unlocked, but display the combination to the safe throughout the lobby. Most businesses and individuals are woefully negligent in not *identifying* and *protecting* their trade secrets; the two initial steps required to turn those assets into dollars.

Many of the subjects discussed in this book are—or should be—of equal interest to both employers and employees. This includes Chapter 1, which defines "proprietary information," and Chapter 2, which describes the general strategies for protecting proprietary information, patent, copyright, and trade secret. Chapter 4 discusses two of the most common types of trade secret disputes, improper use of customer lists and "raiding" of employees. And Chapter 6 deals with the fascinating, frustrating, and expensive world of lawsuits over trade secrets. Employers will be especially interested in Chapter 3, which lists specific techniques for protecting trade secrets. However, employees who have the ambition to become employers should cover this material as well. Finally, "peripatetic" employees, itching to get started in their own ventures, will certainly be most interested in Chapter 5, which lays out the how-to's of going into business in competition with your former employer. However, this one should not be ignored by the employer who wants to know what plots are hatching in the lunchroom.

HUMMEL

1
What is Proprietary Information?

Not knowing what constitutes proprietary information was certainly one way many entrepreneurs may have lost their valuable technology in the past. Although the following is a hypothetical story, it is representative of the learning process that many have faced in their early struggles with information protection.

At Electron Products, Ed Pascal was a technical genius. He created the company's most important product, and continued to lead an ambitious research and development program. Like many engineers, Ed was fiercely proud of his work, and had been logging his daily brainstorms, complete with sketches and meeting notes, in a series of notebooks. In his career, he had worked for four companies, taking his expanding library with him on each move. He commanded a lot of respect from his co-workers, and had personally recruited many of them from his last job. Ed had been with Electron for three years.

Dick Tindall also worked at Electron as its regional marketing director. He had been with the company longer than Ed, almost from the beginning, and had contributed to its excellent sales growth. His performance was motivated largely by a commission plan, which had paid him handsomely in the last couple of years, once he had struggled through the start-up phase. Recently, however, management revised the commission plan. In plain terms, he was making too much money. His sales quota was increased, and greater increases were implied to keep his overall compensation "within reason."

As Dick was becoming disenchanted with the ever-advancing carrot at the end of the stick, Ed was shocked to find one of his most significant product proposals rejected by his new manager, Stan Holland, in favor of an idea advanced by a crony brought along by Stan from his last employer. The decision was a bold move by Stan, whose department had recently missed some critical goals, to prove himself to his superiors.

Ed and Dick had often engaged in the kind of idle talk that occurs at after-hours company functions, discussing their thoughts about controlling their own destinies or getting a bigger piece of the action. Now, the talk became more serious. Each decided the time had come to leave and start a business in competition with Electron. After all, Ed was an expert in his field, and knew that his rejected idea was a real winner. To the extent Dick understood it, he agreed, and felt that with the industry connections he had built up over the years, he could easily sell the product. With this initial success, the inevitable growth of their new enterprise could be staffed with the best people now working for them at Electron.

They both left their jobs, taking with them not only their experience and talent, but also Ed's notebooks and Dick's Rolodex of the business contacts he had developed. Neither had signed any contract with Electron. Therefore, they were astounded to be served with a lawsuit alleging their "theft" of Electron's "trade secrets" and "proprietary information." The litigation had been instigated by Stan, who was concerned that some of Ed's friends might leave to join the new company, and who needed a convenient scapegoat for his department's recent failings. The legal fight was extremely bitter. Each side incurred expensive legal fees and lost invaluable time. In the end, there was no real winner. Other competition, undiverted by legal battles, overtook them both.

Although this grim, frustrating account is not true, it is an amalgam of several real "trade secret" cases. Both sides entered litigation and lost to each other because they were basically ignorant on the subject of "proprietary information." Electron had never established a system to identify and protect the basic technology and business information which it needed to keep secret from the outside world. And Ed and Dick never considered whether what they took away on paper and in their heads was really theirs to take.

This book provides the basic education needed to keep employers and employees out of court on these disputes, or, where that is not possible, to prepare them for the fight and maximize their chances of winning it. Since the fight concerns proprietary information, exploring what that means is of primary importance.

Definition

Generally speaking, proprietary information is simply "commercially useful" ideas. We are not concerned here with novelty or obviousness; considerations which arise with patents. However, if you expect anything to be "proprietary," whether it is technological data or customer information, it must at least not be generally known. The phrase "commercially useful" is used here to mean eliminating information of academic interest only. That distinction may be obvious, however, since most innovators probably spend little time on nonprofitable information. Capitalism has a way of turning most good ideas into money, if properly treated.

If you run a business, proprietary information or intellectual property consists of any data that helps sell your product, or increase your revenues or profits. A chemical formula, a manufacturing process, a customer list, or an analysis of your competition, suggest just a few examples. From an individual's point of view, proprietary information refers to anything that embodies an idea which you can sell to a business, or turn into a business.

Whether you make potato chips or silicon chips, whether you sell soap or computer time, you probably own far more proprietary information than you think. The most seemingly trivial things can qualify. The method you use for figuring your bids or running your conveyor belts, or your knowledge of an important customer's favorite cigar, may seem relatively unimportant to you. You may have spent little or no money or effort obtaining the information. Indeed, you may have discovered it by chance. However, it is yours, and it gives you an advantage over your competition. Unless you're in the unusual position of being a monopoly, you can't afford to dissipate that asset by giving it away to your competitors, or by simply letting it rot in your "inventory."

Technology and Business Information

Proprietary information includes *technology* and *business information.* These categories reflect the distinct problems or opportunities that arise in this area. Also, this division is helpful once you have identified your proprietary information and begun to consider the most appropriate methods of protecting and utilizing it.

Technology may consist of a machine, design, formula, or method of manufacture. You may already understand what constitutes patentable material. However, don't be confused. Although all patentable matter falls generally within the "technology" category of proprietary information, the reverse is not true. In fact, an enormous universe of ideas (such as "know-how") is not patentable, but can qualify as proprietary information. And that universe expands daily. Proprietary technology is distinguished from business information in part by its general application to a class of businesses. Examples include a method for mixing structural concrete, an electronic circuit diagram, computer software, and a chef's pastry recipe.

Proprietary business information specifies how you make and plan to make money. While it does not necessarily apply to other businesses, knowing it could help them compete more effectively against your business. Examples include an employee list, a customer list, a description of employee benefits, and a marketing plan.

Stop reading for at least five or ten minutes and recall some less obvious examples of these two general areas in your own business. As soon as possible, assemble an exhaustive list of the technology and business information which is proprietary to your business or department. Remember that "proprietary" means it is yours. However, it does not have to be exclusively yours, as long as it is not widely known like a principle of physics or mathematics. Consider, also, that many otherwise obvious or generally known ideas may be part of a unique or unusual combination which your proprietary information contains.

Unfortunately, there are no consulting services available to help you identify your intellectual property assets. However, reading this book should develop your understanding of the subject.

Identifying Your Proprietary Information

Review your company, division, or department and analyze what you make or provide and how you go about making and marketing it. Then consider methodologies that may differ from your competition and the data or processes you would not want the competition to have or know. Next, break this technology and business information into categories. Develop an inventory scheme for your business. Join your other managers and direct them to perform the same analysis.

The first step of identifying your proprietary information is the most difficult one. You will use this analysis to formulate and implement a policy for protecting, exploiting, and maximizing the usefulness of your trade secrets. More likely than not, you will be light-years ahead of your competition. Several of the largest "high-technology" firms in the "Silicon Valley" of Northern California have not performed this analysis. If you don't do it, you are at best being inefficient; at worst, you run a substantial risk of losing your most important assets.

Ownership

Of course, as you list the things you own, you must develop some method of deciding what really does belong to you. This issue arises almost exclusively with respect to technology. Often the question involves the rights of the employer versus the employee concerning an invention that the employee has made. This is a critical question if you are an employee who has developed a product or process in your spare time, and now wonder how to capitalize on it without losing your job or getting sued.

In general (the specific laws vary from state to state), three situations are possible. They reflect the nature of the employee's duties and what is used to develop the invention. First, if the employee is *hired to invent*, and the discovery falls within the assigned work area, then the idea will normally belong to the employer, since the invention simply fulfilled the job requirements.

Second, if the employee was not hired to invent, or if the discovery is outside the scope of the assigned duties, but the employer's resources are used to produce the invention, then the employer has a *shop right* to the idea. This is the equivalent of a non-exclusive, royalty-free license to use, but not to sell the idea. The employee has all remaining rights to the idea. Thus, a stock room clerk who discovers a new and more efficient type of pallet will own the rights to that invention, subject to the employer's shop right.

Finally, when the employee discovers an invention without using the employer's resources, and it is not considered within the "hired" duties, the invention belongs exclusively to the employee. However, this assumes that the employee developed the invention without using any trade secrets or other proprietary information belonging to the employer. This is distinct from the "resources" referenced in connection with the shop right which consists of the non-unique, tangible assets of the employer, such as raw materials, time, facilities, and so on. So, if an employee creates an invention which either incorporates or in some way uses the employer's exclusive, proprietary data, then the issue of ownership is less clear and requires legal assistance to unravel.

The issue of ownership may also be affected by special rules or statutes peculiar to individual states. In California, for example, a recently enacted law provides that employees retain all rights to any invention created on their own time without use of their employer's facilities or proprietary information.

Contracts can also make a difference. A properly worded employment contract can require an employee to assign all inventions, patentable or not, that are created during the employment period. However, the construction and enforceability of such contracts vary from state to state and you will probably require some legal advice if this issue applies to you.

A final point relates to the widespread misconception that individuals "own" whatever is in their heads. This is not true; an employer's proprietary information, whether it is a customer list or a secret manufacturing process, cannot be used by the employee after terminating employment, even if the information is unwritten and stored in the employee's head. However, an employee can keep and freely use any general knowledge or skills acquired on the job. Like many distinctions, this one is far easier to state than it is to apply. Nevertheless, this standard is almost universally used in deciding what information exclusively belongs to the employer, and what information the employee may take and use. How this concept is applied to the more common areas of dispute between employer and former employee will be explored in some detail in subsequent chapters.

HUMMEL
TRADE SECRET
PATENT
C

2
Methods of Protection

If you have successfully performed the steps outlined in Chapter 1, then you now know what proprietary information you possess. You also know that it's an important asset, one which is rapidly deteriorating in value as you read these words. At worst, your information can disappear entirely, if you don't protect it from use by others.

You've probably recognized the basic dilemma in marketing an idea without giving others access to it. If so, then as the psychiatrists say, you have solved half of the problem by recognizing that it exists. In this chapter we will deal with the three recognized methods of protecting your intellectual property: *patent*, *copyright*, and *trade secret*.

First, we will survey each method and generally define what it protects and how each method works. Trade secret protection is treated more extensively than the other methods; the concept is not taken from a statute, making it more difficult to define. Further, the trade secret method of protection is becoming more widely used throughout the industry. In the following section, we will explore some of the reasons for that trend, comparing the pros and cons of trade secret protection with those of patent and copyright. Finally, we will consider the specific problems of protecting the employed or self-employed individual's commercially useful ideas.

Patents

The government grants a patent to an inventor (or to the person or company designated by the inventor) to *legally monopolize* the use of a specific invention for a limited time. More precisely, a patent stipulates the right to prevent or exclude others from making or using the invention. Unlike trade secrets, the basic idea underlying patents is disclosure to the public. Disclosure is presumably safe because for a certain period, you obtain the sole right to use or sell the invention. This right is defined and governed by United States statutes. Through well-established procedures, you can secure a declaration from the government that the invention is yours.

As expressed by Congress, the intent of the patent laws is to encourage innovation by the individual inventor, while making the invention "available" to the public. This availability takes two dimensions. First, through license or assignment the public can buy the invention or a right to use it from you. Second, this public knowledge may help others to innovate further by stimulating new and different inventions. Of course, all of this commerce and inventiveness helps grease the wheels of progress.

The Process

Qualifying your idea as a patent, however, is not a simple process. First, you must consider whether your invention constitutes patentable subject matter. Patents may be granted for "new and useful processes, machines, manufactured articles, compositions of matter of plants" (35 United States Code and 101). The U.S. Supreme Court has been allowed a patent to be issued on an artificially produced bacterium. So, life itself is patentable. As defined by the patent laws, "utility" only qualifies whether the invention works, not whether it is commercially useful. However, business information, as we previously described it, and "know-how" are not patentable.

Other hurdles you must jump in qualifying your patent include novelty and "non-obviousness." The invention must be something that is truly new, not something "suggested" by other patents or technology already in use (referred to as "prior art"). To ascertain your position, you must extensively search the patent files to determine whether your invention differs from prior technology, or whether it infringes on some earlier patent. Like many other apparently simple concepts, "obviousness" is difficult to understand and often subjective in its partial application. The patent office may find your invention is so distinct from existing practice that it is not obvious to a person skilled in your field. Yet, the whole issue can be decided conversely in later litigation with an accused infringer or a licensee determined to escape royalty payments.

Nevertheless, because of the relatively uniform way of establishing and recognizing patents, certain people assign a special value to patented inventions. Thus, if you plan to sell your invention, or a right to use it, to someone else, rather than to exploit it yourself, you should consider patent protection. Since patent rights are well-defined, and represent a clear monopoly position for a definite time period, companies pay hard dollars more often for patent rights than for any other type of intellectual property.

If you are working on an invention that you may want patented, then you must begin patent application procedures without delay. A patent application must be filed within one year of the first commercial use of the invention. First, prepare a rough drawing or written description of the invention, date it and have it witnessed, preferably by two trusted friends or associates. It is a well-established habit of engineers and inventors to graphically describe their ideas in bound notebooks which they sign, date, and periodically have witnessed. In fact, if you employ people for invention purposes, it is a good practice to require them to keep such records, and to account for and turn in the notebooks when they terminate employment.

Beyond properly authenticating the discovery which comprises your invention, you must consult with a well-qualified patent attorney for more detailed information about the cost, time, and effort involved in prosecuting the patent. This adviser will provide invaluable assistance in drafting the specific claims which define the boundaries of your invention, as well as conducting the required patent search. Be sure to cooperate completely with your representative. Don't hesitate to disclose or explain every aspect of your invention. The patent attorney is required to keep such information confidential and simply cannot perform effectively without knowing all of the necessary information.

Risks and Responsibilities

Patents do not guarantee instant, abundant wealth or even a basic meal ticket. As many professional inventors will confide, most patents are never used. They are not purchased or licensed because the capital necessary to develop them cannot be found. And a patent can be ruled invalid by a court, even though the Patent Office examiners have passed on its sufficiency. Further, in spite of the depth and breadth of the search you make, prior art might later be found to invalidate your patent. You could wind up paying expensive legal fees with absolutely nothing to show for it.

Even if the patent is secure against other claims, your government-granted monopoly is not policed by the United States; that is your job. By whatever means are available to you or your licensee, you must discover and prosecute infringers of your patent. Discovering infringers can be difficult, particularly of "process" patents, since the final, manufactured item does not easily reveal how it was made. This is equally true of most computer software, which explains why more people are not pushing for its direct coverage under the patent laws. And even when you unearth the offending party, pursuing the case will certainly be expensive and may be completely unproductive.

If you want to learn more about patents, the following publications are available from the U.S. Department of Commerce Patent and Trademark Office, or may be purchased through the U.S. Superintendent of Documents: "Patents, Inventions: An Information Aid for Inventors" and "General Information Concerning Patents."

Copyright

Copyright protects only the *form* in which you express an idea, *not* the idea itself. This is what distinguishes copyright from both the patent and trade secret (which protect the substance of the invention or information). For example, throughout this book there are probably some original ideas, which now belong to you and to everyone who reads this book. You are all free to use them. However, if you were to *express* those ideas in a publication, by using the same words and phrases used here, you would be in violation of the copyright covering this book.

Therefore, copyright protection is appropriate when you wish to protect the *form*. Among the many paradoxes that exist in the law of intellectual property, form often becomes substance, since the form is most important to the creator. This is frequently true for drawings, blueprints, and the like. For other types of intellectual property, form becomes important because it provides the most convenient and effective means of judging whether someone has stolen the fruits of the creative effort. This is most often true of literary works, music, and computer software.

For most types of technology and business information, however, copyright is *not* the appropriate form of protection. It is not the means of expressing the idea, but rather the idea itself, you need to protect. In fact, many professionals justifiably contend that placing a copyright notice on a document implies publication to the world. This is inconsistent with trade secret protection, and may cost you your trade secret status.

Like patent laws, the copyright statutes provide a type of monopoly over use of the form, and this protection may best suit your technology. For example, the 1980 amendments to the Copyright Act clearly allow copyrighting computer programs. Where mass marketing of these programs make trade secret protection (by contract) impractical, copyright registration may be the best available alternative.

There is no longer "common law" copyright. Under the 1976 Copyright Act which became effective in 1978, all copyright matters are governed by federal statute. That statute is found in 17 United States Code sections 101-810. It gives the owner of a copyright (whether published or not) the exclusive right to sell, reproduce, or prepare derivative works from the copyrighted material. Like patents, the owner of a copyright may be the person for whom the material was prepared (for example, an employer). Also like patents, a copyright may be assigned or sold, although this must be done in writing. The term of protection generally extends for the life of the author, plus 50 years.

The Process

To ensure copyright protection for publicly distributed copies, you must display the following information on each copy of the work:

- The symbol ©
- The year of first publication
- The name of the copyright owner.

The statute requires the owner to deposit two copies of the work with the Register of Copyrights in Washington, D.C., within three months of publication. However, this requirement does not apply to technical drawings or machine-readable data. The validity of the copyright is not affected by failure to deposit. The statute also describes how to register the work and secure a determination by the Copyright Office that the material can be copyrighted. Registration is not required to validate the copyright, although a finding by the Copyright Office determining copyrightability is helpful in court. If you register the work prior to an infringement of your copyright, you may sue an infringer for attorney's fees and statutory penalties, up to $50,000. If you are concerned about public access to the material while registration is pending, consult with the Copyright Office. Several types of submissions may be kept confidential and returned after copyrightability has been determined.

Trade Secrets

Unlike patents and copyrights, the concept of trade secrets is not a creation of the statute books. Moreover, because it is defined separately by each state, the law of trade secrets will vary from one jurisdiction to another. (A Uniform Trade Secrets Act has been proposed to the states, but has yet to be adopted.) Trade secret law has been created by the courts in an effort to establish rules for "fair competition" among businesses. And because of its judicial genesis, it is flexible enough to cover an enormous range of ideas, inventions, and other business information.

A trade secret is often generally defined as any formula, pattern, device, or compilation of information used in a business that gives the owner an advantage over competitors who neither know of or use it. Although this description is necessarily vague, keep in mind that your own trade secrets should be reasonably specific. You must be able to describe what it is that you claim as as a trade secret. Without a precise description, you cannot prepare an appropriate plan to protect it or expect others to respect your rights. Moreover, the courts will not recognize trade secret claims that are not sufficiently specific.

As you might conclude from this definition, almost anything can qualify as a trade secret, from complex circuit designs to Colonel Sanders' "secret blend of 11 herbs and spices." Examples of trade secrets the courts have recognized include

- A soft drink formula (for example, Coca-Cola™; its formula is perhaps the most famous trade secret).
- A rat poison formula.

- A process for extracting alcohol from empty whisky barrels.
- A method of flavoring mouthwash.
- A process of manufacturing orchestral cymbals (this one has been maintained as a secret within one family for hundreds of years).
- The seminar technique of a group nonsmoking clinic.
- Designs for automatic toll collection equipment.
- Customer lists.
- Computer software.
- New product plans.
- Advertising plans.
- Cost and pricing data.
- Employee benefit information.

A trade secret also differs from a patent or a copyright, since the idea or invention represented need not be unique to the owner. Several competitors in the same market might each have come to possess the same trade secret through independent development. It is a factual question whether a trade secret may become a commonly known industry practice over time, in which case the trade secret status is lost.

An idea need not be patentable in order to receive trade secret protection. Nor is novelty a strict requirement, although some courts are more likely to grant protection to a novel invention. This is especially true in cases where no demonstrable fraud or breach of trust exists. This is the important distinction: a trade secret is not limited to patentable subject matter (machines, processes, compositions of material, and articles of manufacture), but extends to cover virtually the entire range of "know-how" and business practices.

How the Courts Rule

How do you know whether your information qualifies as a trade secret? Although the definition provided at the beginning of this section is the best shorthand answer, the courts consider several factors in deciding whether any given item of intellectual property qualifies. These factors are posed in the following questions:

How extensively was the matter disclosed in a patent?

To that extent, it is normally deemed public information and the courts will not prohibit others from using it. This is critical if you are considering seeking patent protection for certain portions of your technology while treating the remainder as trade secrets. Patent applications must be written with enough detail to enable a person of ordinary skill in the field to duplicate the invention just by reading the patent. If you omit information necessary to describe the invention's "best mode of use," you may invalidate any patent you receive. For instance, you might describe a broad temperature range in a process, when you know the best results are obtained in a specific, narrower range. But the more information you include, the more likely you are to compromise the trade secret status of details you wish to maintain as a secret. This potential dilemma requires close and continuing attention in the management of your intellectual property. Of course, while the patent is pending (two to three years), you still have your trade secret protection. It is only lost when the patent is granted and published.

How extensively is the information known outside your company?
This is an extremely critical factor. In the best circumstance, of course, proprietary information is not known at all. However, it is frequently necessary to reveal proprietary information to customers, vendors, the government, and others. Even if strict measures have been taken to prevent wholesale distribution of the information, the fact that several sources outside the company know it, reflects negatively. As a general rule, the more the information has been distributed, the more protective measures a court will want to see adopted before conferring trade secret status.

How extensively is the information known among employees within the company?
At one end of the spectrum, a manufacturer maintains a secret formula by imparting distinct portions of the formula to a few trusted employees. At the other end, a business makes otherwise secret information accessible to large numbers of employees, none of whom could adequately justify their need to know.

What measures have been taken to guard the secrecy of the information?
This is the single most important consideration. Significant amounts of time, energy, and money are invested to determine whether the secret holder took reasonable steps to protect the secret from unauthorized disclosure or use. Virtually all of the material described in Chapter 3 is relevant to this issue. However, qualification for trade secret protection does not require running your business like the Central Intelligence Agency. Instead, the court applies a more flexible standard; "reasonable" measures must be taken to protect the information. As a general rule, the more important and sensitive the information is, the greater the protection effort required for trade secret status to apply.

How easily can the information be independently acquired or duplicated? This often becomes the critical factor in a "customer list" case, where the former employee is charged with unfair solicitation of the former employer's customers. The perfect defense would show how you created your own list from scratch, using publicly available sources (for more on this, see Chapter 4).

With respect to manufactured articles, the courts will consider whether it can be "reverse-engineered." In technology trade secret cases, a sufficient defense shows that you developed a similar article simply by disassembling the plaintiff's product to determine its components and design. The underlying idea assumes there is nothing unfair about simply copying what you can see, even if you must disassemble it to do it (assuming, of course, no patent or copyright infringement). Thus, the supposed secret is not really a secret at all. Even if the defendant did not reverse-engineer the article, but "unfairly" developed it by hiring away one of the plaintiff's designers, it is sometimes sufficient to show that the article could have been reverse-engineered. This may convince the judge that the claimed proprietary information was not a real secret. Or, it may result in an injunction against using the secret for the period of time that it would otherwise have taken to reverse-engineer the item.

How much money was spent in developing the information?
The dollar value of the development process is often one of the most significant factors. Although many judges may find many of the concepts of intellectual property difficult and the technology unfamiliar, one thing they all understand is money. If you can demonstrate that an improper use or disclosure of the secret will cost your business tens or hundreds of thousands of dollars in lost revenue, you will have the judge's attention. And if you can show that you spent significant money to develop the secret—an investment which would be lost forever without an injunction—you will almost always have the judge on your side. For your most important, easily identifiable items of intellectual property, maintain an accounting system that will permit you to recover this type of information quickly and accurately.

How novel is the secret?
Although novelty is not a necessary component of a trade secret, in practice it will influence the outcome in a court's decision. Thus, you should examine the uniqueness of your secret, and write the best description of it you can.

How specifically can the secret be described?
Courts normally will not (and should not) issue injunctions against using "ABC Company's trade secrets or confidential information." The phrase is too ambiguous for the defendant to understand what can and cannot be done. Therefore, before you can expect the court to protect your secret, you must be able to clearly articulate what it is.

Does the secret include employee "general knowledge"?

As discussed in Chapter 1, a company's proprietary information does not include the general knowledge possessed by each employee concerning how he or she performs the job. Therefore, you cannot claim this type of information as a trade secret.

How extensively would an injunction inhibit the employee from pursuing a chosen career?

If you required an employee to work almost exclusively with proprietary information, absolute protection of that information would require prohibiting the individual from any subsequent work for competitors. However, the courts are sensitive to the anti-competitive effect of such rulings, since they tend to make an individual defendant essentially unemployable. Do not involve an employee so exclusively in secret work that he or she cannot find any subsequent employment without using it.

If these broad definitions and complex factors have only created more confusion, you have accurately assessed a basic problem of trade secret law: it is extremely difficult to determine exactly what constitutes a trade secret. This difficulty evolves from the courts' attempts to pigeon-hole trade secret law into certain traditional legal fields. For instance, many judges and lawyers first treated the subject as property, and applied rules concerning ownership, definition, and theft of personal property to the developing concepts in intellectual property. Other courts emphasized the confidential relationship between the parties. In fact, such relationships weigh significantly in many cases. Other courts stress contractual obligations against disclosing or using certain information. More recently, many judges have supported the law of trade secret protection as simply an ad hoc effort to enforce commercial morality. Rather than basing protection on outdated or inapplicable principles of contract or property law, many judges realize the history of trade secret litigation requires they follow their own visceral reactions.

This is a positive development. A system that considers all the facts and circumstances in light of certain established but not necessarily controlling principles will be beneficial. With the quickening pace of technological change and the rapid-fire transactions that characterize modern commerce, anything less flexible would not work in the long run. But whether or not you agree, consider a trade secret as a religion; if you believe you have it, and you act as if you have it, then you've probably got it. Remember that metaphor, as it will be discussed later in detail. Appearances often determine who wins or loses a trade secret contest.

Therefore, in qualifying a protectable trade secret, considering how you can make it look is as important as considering what it is.

Patent vs. Trade Secret Protection

Patent protection is inappropriate for many types of intellectual property. Often the information consists of unpatentable subject matter, such as know-how. Moreover, given the increasing rate of technological development, and the increasing volatility of innovations produced, many attorneys who deal with intellectual property prefer the trade secret method of protection to patent under several circumstances. This does not imply a choice in most instances; the nature of the idea often dictates the appropriate form of protection. Review Table 2-1 to understand the differences between the two forms of protection, and to appreciate the reasons for this trend.

To further understand how the requirements for a patent and a trade secret differ, consider the federal court's comments in an early trade secret case. The court noted that a patent requires an "invention" while a trade secret requires simply a "discovery."

> "Quite clearly discovery is something less than invention. Invention requires genius, imagination, inspiration, or whatever is the faculty that gives birth to the inventive concept. Discovery may be the result of industry, application, or be perhaps merely fortuitous . . . "
>
> (*A.O. Smith Corp.* v. *Petroleum Iron Works Co.*, Sixth Circuit U.S. Court of Appeals 1934, 73 F2d 531)

Novelty and Obviousness

One of the drawbacks of patents requires proving to the Patent Office that the invention is novel and not obvious. The patent process involves comparing the idea with a whole body of prior technology. The standards are applied in a vacuum by a corps of Washington technocrats. Conversely, you may "establish" your trade secret simply on the basis of its usefulness and value. Only when you defend it against disclosure or use by others must you support its protectability. When that time comes, a judge will make the decision after considering all the "equities" of the situation (such as how the defendant acquired the information). These equities may

Table 2-1. Comparison of Patent vs. Trade Secret

	Patent	Trade Secret
Subject Matter	Specific and limited by statute (machines, articles of manufacture, processes and composition of matter)	Applies to broad range of intellectual property and business information
Requirements	Must be useful	Must provide competitive advantage
	Must be novel	Must not be generally known
	Must not be obvious	Must be kept secret
Definition	Defined strictly by language of the "claims"	Often difficult to define with equal precision, but can be as broad as the "equities" of a particular case require
Disclosure	Required	Any disclosure must be limited and controlled
Protection	Defined by narrow but specific statute	Varies depending on circumstances and court based on many theories
	Can prohibit use by anyone else	Protection only against "unfair" users; none against those who independently discover or reverse-engineer
Duration	17 years from issuance	Potentially unlimited as long as secret
Expense	Procuring policing infringement	Protecting from unauthorized disclosure or use
Risk	Invalidity	Independent discovery or inadvertent disclosure
Marketability	Licensing easier	Licensing more difficult, and requires policing of licensee security measures

be totally unaffected by the nature of the information or its relationship to prior technology.

Carefully consider the definition of your proprietary information. In order to secure a patent, you must prepare precisely worded "claims" to describe the invention. Once awarded, the patent affords advantages inherent in a government-recognized description of your property. However, the scope of the claims which the Patent Office approves may be narrower than you feel reasonably describes the invention. You may have disclosed the "guts" of your idea and received protection for little of it. Indeed, the Patent Office may not accept any statement of your claims which you find acceptable, making the whole process worthless. Of course, at that point you can abandon the patent application and pursue trade secret protection, assuming the information remained confidential.

By contrast, trade secrets can be extraordinarily broad since they are limited only by vague concepts of usefulness and reasonable secrecy. This necessarily makes trade secrets difficult to define in advance of litigation over their uses. Since the process of identifying and categorizing one's trade secrets is neither standardized nor required by the law, most businesses ignore it. In addition, many feel that any effort to define trade secrets will necessarily exclude others which may exist.

You will learn, as you read further, that it is essential to define your proprietary information. Otherwise, you will be unable to inventory it, and make an intelligent plan for protecting and utilizing it. Moreover, unless you can clearly describe your proprietary information to your employees, your security program will be largely ineffective. Finally, do not be concerned about the negative implications of defining certain things as your trade secrets to the possible exclusion of others. Clearly express to your employees that your "list" or other specification is not necessarily exhaustive. (See Chapter 3, on education and agreements.)

Disclosure

Consider another significant difference between the two types of protection: a patent requires disclosure, while a trade secret inherently requires secrecy. If you can adequately use your intellectual property while maintaining its secrecy, you might at least avoid the problems that accompany disclosure. Chief among these is the potential awakening of the sleeping giant of a "dominating patent" which your patent search did not reveal. The end result may be your inability to use the technology at all. Conversely, under the trade secret method of protection, your supposed infringement might never have been discovered, freeing you to exploit the invention.

Also consider the rights granted by each form of protection. A patent awards exclusive, monopoly rights for a period of 17 years. A trade secret offers a potentially unlimited duration. But, it only protects the secret from those who use it "unfairly," such as those who acquire it through a confidential relationship or who violate an agreement to maintain its secrecy. Your rights are not violated by anyone who can prove acquisition of the trade secret by independent, separate discovery (whether by research or accident), or by reverse-engineering your product which embodies the secret.

With respect to a patent, you are less likely to secure an immediate injunction against the infringer's use of the invention. Often, the courts feel that the potential harm suffered by the infringer's business is too great to justify that kind of relief. Instead, damages are easily determined from sales revenues or other use of the infringing material.

Conversely, with trade secret protection you can get an injunction more easily, since the trade secret status can be lost if any third party uses the information. Therefore in that situation, a court will often focus on whether the potential harm in denying an injunction to the owner outweighs the potential harm to the alleged infringer from issuing an injunction against its use or disclosure.

Expense

As anyone who has secured a patent will tell you, the process is not only slow (the average waiting time is 19 months), but extremely expensive. Once the patent has been granted, the cost of enforcement can be extraordinarily high. It may involve litigation against an infringer, or a dispute with a licensee who benefited from the invention, and claiming patent invalidity, wants to escape payment.

Policing infringement of process patents is especially difficult, since it is virtually impossible to determine how a competitor's finished product was made. If the infringer is smart and careful in protecting process information, you may never discover that the infringement has occurred. This is why the computer industry has not enthusiastically embraced patenting computer software. As with a process, you cannot easily determine whether software has been copied from other software. At the same time, most applications software can be relatively easily reverse-engineered, favoring copyright over trade secret protection.

Trade secret protection is also not without substantial expense. As the material covered in Chapter 3 demonstrates, taking security measures to protect proprietary data can be expensive. However, because the courts require only reasonable protection in granting trade secret status, you may tailor your security program to the type of secrets involved, investing funds accordingly. Moreover, a well-designed security program applies to all proprietary information, including both business data and technology, and the cost can therefore be shared among several company assets.

Risks

With a patent, though you've spent the necessary funds to secure and enforce protection, you always run the risk that a court will invalidate the patent, or will cite your infringement on a prior, dominating patent. Such a finding might apply to all your applications of the invention.

In choosing trade secret protection, you risk losing the secret through inadvertent disclosure, inadequate security, or independent discovery. The first of these potential problems lies largely within your own control; if you have taken reasonable measures to protect your proprietary information, the court will prevent another from using it, and may even "call back" accidentally disclosed information. As for the risk of independent discovery, you can only guess whether or when that might occur. However, the new discoverer(s) might also keep it secret, permitting you to treat it as a "shared" secret, protected from everyone else.

Also, a court may find your information does not meet the requirements of a trade secret at all. However, trade secret litigation considers the peculiar circumstances of each case; such a determination would not affect the validity of your trade secret claims in any other case.

Remember, the importance of your proprietary information depends on how much money it makes. You can sell or license the technology rather than use it yourself to create products or services. Many people find licensing a patent easier than licensing a trade secret. Prospective buyers are familiar with patents, and the limited governmental guarantee of its value. A well-established method deals with patents as property. Further, the rigid definition of an invention covered by a patent usually makes it easier to understand, and therefore value its possible applications.

Conversely, trade secrets are not so easily defined and do not come with the government's stamp of approval. Moreover, licensing a trade secret normally will require you to spend time and money in policing the licensee's security measures for protecting the data against other unauthorized use or disclosure. Nevertheless, trade secrets have been successfully licensed, sometimes for enormous sums of money. You and your prospective licensees should consider the unique nature of the secret and the ability of everyone involved to adequately protect it by contract and other security measures.

Licenses and Agreements

An important distinction between patents and trade secrets regards licenses. A licensee may attempt to escape royalty obligations by proving that the patent was invalidly issued. Many people presume that the same rule applies to transfers of technology protected as trade secrets, and that third-party disclosure or discovery of the information will excuse royalty payments. Consider the following case.

The owner of an invention decided to license the technology which was protected as a trade secret while the patent was pending. The patent application was eventually denied and the information became public. As a result of the court's ruling, the licensee, who once enjoyed exclusive right to the invention, now became the only one in the industry required to pay for using it. However, in ruling on this recent case, the federal appellate court found that the licensee had effectively assumed that risk, and refused to excuse further royalties. Therefore, if you are considering a potential acquisition of technology, you may be taking more risk in acquiring a trade secret than a patent. If your patent license fee is supposed to run for five years, but after the first year you prove the patent invalid, you can then use the invention without cost. However, your obligation to pay a royalty under a trade secret license will last the entire contract term and you "assume the risk" that the trade secret may enter the public domain.

One final problem with patents is that you must define not only the invention, but also the inventor or inventors. By law, patents are prosecuted not in the name of the owner but in the name of the individual inventor. Determining exactly who that individual is or whether others may have contributed to the invention is a potential headache (a patent might be found invalid simply for naming too few or too many inventors). Under trade secret protection, identifying single or multiple inventors is not a problem since the focus is on the owner of the trade secret.

Of course, in the patent area it is important to secure an agreement from all employees to assign ownership in their inventions to the company. Obtain written declarations from employees who have been hired to invent confirming their job-related inventions belong to the company. Chapter 3 covers these matters in more detail, and introduces the forms of employee agreements which appear in the Appendices.

Trade secret protection is not necessarily better than patent in all circumstances. There are many good reasons to seek a patent. Generally, the facts listed above may favor patenting the particular property requiring protection. And your inventor-employees may be more motivated by a potential patent. Although assigned to the company, a patent bears the employees' names and imparts a degree of prestige. That prestige may benefit the company, affecting its ability to recruit qualified employees or to raise funds by identifying patent "assets."

Remember, too, you can secretly apply for a patent while retaining the trade secret status of your idea. Therefore, if the scope of the allowed claims is too narrow or if the claims are totally denied, you could continue treating the matter as a trade secret. In addition, your patent application need not disclose all of the technology related to the patent. Although the law requires a thorough description of the invention, it is not unusual to concurrently maintain significant trade secrets which are directly related to the invention you seek to patent. Examples include process information, uses of the invention, and equipment necessary to make it. Be cautious here, however, since the statute requires that the patent application disclose the "best mode" of the invention. If you hold back this information on the application, the patent may later be invalidated. The difficulty of drawing the line here, between disclosing more than required and withholding something which may defeat the whole effort, can itself be a drawback to the patent process.

Overall, you must determine the best way to protect and exploit your proprietary information. In addition to the patent and trade secret alternatives, you should consider the possibility of copyright protection.

Copyright vs. Trade Secret

It is easier to decide whether to use the copyright form of protection since it applies to a more limited area of intellectual property. As previously noted, the copyright laws protect only the *form* of expression of your ideas, while trade secret protection extends to the idea itself.

There may be two reasons to use copyright protection for your proprietary information. First, copyright protects against copying by *anyone*, regardless of any relationship with the owner. Conversely, in trade secret law, the existence of a confidential relationship in which the knowledge is acquired and the promise of confidentiality is implied, is a central fact. Second, in practice a copyright notice normally tends to discourage pilferage of ideas as well as format. It's like the "electronic alarm system" sign on your front window. The prospective thief presumes if you have invested that much energy you probably will make things messy for him. And easier touches abound elsewhere.

So, in addition to the forms of trade secret protection outlined in Chapter 3, you may consider using a copyright notice on your internal documentation and on any drawings and handbooks you supply to customers. (Proceed cautiously, however, as many lawyers believe a copyright notice on *any* document destroys potential trade secret protection; the implied "publication" conflicts with secrecy, and the new federal copyright law may "preempt" state trade secret law. However, copyright protection can be used on trade secret documents with limited circulation. Consult your own counsel on this point.

Do not throw away the trade secret protection you need through publication. Remember, copyright does not simply substitute for trade secret protection; in certain circumstances it may be a useful supplement, but it must be used with care.

Certain technologies must be widely published to realize the potential economic benefits. For this type of intellectual property, copyright protection may be particularly useful. For example, consider computer software. Regaining the large investment necessary to develop this technology often requires extensive distribution. Yet it's impractical to enforce contractual limitations on thousands of consumers. Although trade secret protection through contractual agreements with purchasers and licensed users should be considered, copyright registration may be the most useful, primary mode of protection in this situation.

Copyright programs demand the same level of attention to detail as do trade secrets. In a recent appellate case, the manufacturer of a "computerized" chess game lost its copyright protection. Some early games were sold to the public without a copyright notice on the internal read-only memory chip. The trial court had ruled simply that "machine-readable" software was not copyrightable. (Congress has since enacted the 1980 revision to the Copyright Act, and expressly covered computer software.) Under the 1976 Copyright Act revision, protection is not automatically lost by inadvertent distribution of a relatively small number of copies. However, the above court decision highlights the need for careful controls when you employ *any* form of proprietary information protection.

Compared to the two main statutory forms of data protection (copyright and patent) trade secret is clearly the most useful and flexible. Classifying and treating intellectual property as trade secrets is becoming the most popular way to manage these assets. However, use the inventory process to consider each piece of proprietary data, and decide how best to treat it. This decision essentially depends on how you intend to exploit the data. After reviewing your known proprietary information and determining the best method of protecting each piece, assign someone to follow up the policing efforts on that data, and to create and maintain a system which immediately considers these issues for new innovations. Whether the responsibility falls on you, on a staff members, or on a "technology committee," the issues must be regularly addressed by those with permanent responsibility to do so.

Protecting the Individual's Idea

Let's assume you are an employee, and have come up with a bright idea, an innovation, which you feel is commercially useful. First you must consider who owns it. Review the distinctions presented in Chapter 1 between employees who are hired to invent and those who aren't; and between innovations that relate to the employer's business and those that do not. If you are uncertain, consult a qualified lawyer before taking any steps that may compromise your position. Cooperate with the attorney completely and disclose all important data, particularly any employment agreement or invention assignment contract. And do it promptly, since your right to protection for the idea may depend on taking certain immediate actions.

If your employer does not own the innovation, then your primary concern must be to extensively research its potential value, while disclosing the idea to as few people as possible. Consult a trusted friend who knows the business in which your invention might be applied or locate a qualified, reputable consultant who has specific business experience in the field. When dealing with consultants, it is acceptable and expected to request a nondisclosure agreement denying the consultant use of the idea. (Adapt the model agreement found in Appendix H.) Seek advice extensively; your decisions will require an intelligent assessment of the innovation's *business value*. Without that information, you could spin your wheels and spend enormous sums of money on a useless exercise. On the other hand, if insufficiently aware of the potentially profitable applications, you might dispose of it for less than it is worth or not use it at all.

Although you might find reputable "invention" or "patent promotion" firms, many have reputations as rip-off artists with low success rates and will gladly promote essentially useless ideas for a fee. Get help from someone who has demonstrated a track record of real success in marketing your type of innovation. Unless you have the time to thoroughly investigate such organizations, you may be better off staying completely clear of them.

Another tempting, yet potentially bottomless pit to drop your idea into is the large corporation. Most companies, and especially those involved in technology, energy, and the like, daily receive scores of unsolicited ideas. Most will not even review such submissions unless you sign a strongly worded document granting them permission to examine the technology closely without any obligation to you. It is highly unlikely you will succeed by this route, unless you have devised an extremely specific but useful application for that company.

In summary, beware of apparently "pat" solutions. Keep your idea as close to you as possible. Work hard to gather information from people who know a great deal about the application business. Then seriously consider whether you want to exploit the idea by selling it to someone else, or by going into business for yourself. The latter course is fraught with many hazards. Think long and hard before risking your creativity and industry to become another statistic of inventors who tried to be businessmen and failed. If, on the other hand, you follow the former course, your most important step will be to secure trusted legal and business advisers who will help you properly protect and exploit your idea.

SECRETS
SECRETS
SECRETS
HUMMEL

3
Protecting Trade Secrets

Once you decide that a trade secret protection program is needed, determining what components are required to make the program legally sound is another tough process. An early case, *Motorola, Inc.* v. *Fairchild Camera and Instrument Corp.* (D. Ariz. 1973, 336 F. Supp. 1173), set a general precedent in illustrating what elements the courts may interpret as being essential to trade secret protection.

It began in 1968 when eight executives left the Semiconductor Division of Motorola to join one of Motorola's most significant competitors, Fairchild Semiconductor. The group included several luminaries in the semiconductor industry, including Wilf Corrigan, subsequent president and chairman of Fairchild. Motorola immediately filed a lawsuit against Fairchild and the employees, claiming they had engaged in a conspiracy to steal its trade secrets.

The trial occurred four years later. On behalf of Motorola, a group of lawyers presented testimony from more than 70 witnesses and introduced more than 1500 exhibits into evidence. Then, at Fairchild's request, the judge dismissed the case, finding that each Motorola employee had left Motorola autonomously, without unfair inducement from Fairchild, and without violating any employment contract. More importantly, however, the court denied any help to Motorola because it had failed to take reasonable steps to protect its own trade secrets. Specifically, the court determined the following:

- Although each employee had signed a nondisclosure agreement covering information "which is of a confidential or secret nature," the company never made any effort to tell the employees what that information was. (The judge remarked, "indeed, the conclusion is inevitable that Motorola did not know what [its secrets were] . . . . [t]here was no list or index of any kind in existence in Motorola's records . . . as to what [it] considered to be a proprietary trade secret.")

- Most of the "trade secrets" claimed by Motorola were either revealed in its products, disclosed by patents, generally known to persons skilled in the industry, or otherwise easily available from published literature.

- Motorola regularly conducted tours of its entire production line where it manufactured the items now claimed to be trade secrets. The judge observed,

> "There were no signs in the area warning of trade secrets, no warnings given to those taking the tours, and no statements regarding nondisclosure agreements required to be signed or acknowledged. Persons taking the tour could observe, time, and inquire of operators as to the speed of machine operations and receive honest answers; could operate one of the 'secret' machines and observe its 'secret' process in a separate microscope placed there for this purpose."

This case demonstrates three important points. First, your program for trade secret protection must be carefully conceived and policed. Second, you must constantly seek to *define* your trade secrets. Third, it is *appearances* that count in court; you must make the judge or jury believe you value your trade secrets as though they were the crown jewels.

Appearances are important because your objective is not simply to prevent theft. If someone wants your secrets badly enough, they will find a way to appropriate them. Most companies cannot afford "Fort Knox" security to protect every piece of proprietary information, particularly information that is used daily. However, even if someone succeeds in stealing your trade secrets, you may challenge their right to use them and win, if you can show the "reasonable steps" you took to protect them.

How much protection is necessary? That depends on what you need to protect, and the relative cost of the protection. Motorola certainly did not do enough. And the courts have denied trade secret claims to plaintiffs who failed to post and maintain appropriate guard personnel, or to construct locked and fenced areas, left drawings on the floor or in trash containers, or failed to limit employee or visitor access to particularly sensitive areas of a facility. On the other hand, you certainly can't eliminate every possible avenue of access to your secrets which a persistent thief might find.

In another case, DuPont was given an injunction against aerial photography of a DuPont plant under construction. Although areas of the construction site open to plain view from the air revealed some secret processes, the court said that DuPont was not required to construct an "impenetrable fortress" which would be effective against all conceivable forms of espionage. A more recent decision has clarified the general standard:

> "While absolute secrecy is not required, there must be a substantial element of secrecy so that a third person would have difficulty in acquiring the necessary information for manufacturing the product without resorting to the use of improper means of acquiring the secret."
> (*Clark* v. *Bunker,* Ninth Circuit U.S. Court of Appeals 1972, 453 F2d 1006)

Develop a Protection Program

Effective trade secret protection, like other business endeavors, requires a plan. Design your plan for the type of confidential information you need to protect. Your plan should achieve three goals:

- Prevent theft.
- Discourage theft by establishing the value of your trade secrets and the difficulty of stealing them, as well as the fact that any unauthorized user will face prosecution.
- Maximize the appearance of your program as one designed to meet the first two goals.

Involve everyone in the initial effort. Employees from marketing, engineering, production, personnel, strategic planning, and every major department should help define what needs protection and suggest appropriate ways to protect it. One manager with sufficient experience and expertise to assess relative needs and costs of protection should be in charge of this program.

Seek Potential Leaks

The extent of the program you design will reflect the company's size, the type of technology and business information you need to protect, the rate of employee turnover, past experience with theft of secrets, the potential impact of unauthorized use or disclosure of your information, and any other particular circumstance that affects the cost and usefulness of each method. In assessing those factors, consider the possible sources of "leaks" of confidential information. These include

- Employees (especially those who are on the way out).
- Vendors (especially their sales representatives).
- Fabricators and subcontractors (who may have inadequate security at their facilities or who may be asked by a competitor to manufacture a similar product).
- Published articles by employees.
- Trade shows, advertisements, and other promotional material.
- Customers.
- Visitors (for example, tours).
- Licensees (and prospective licensees)[1].
- Government (for example, an Occupational Safety and Hazard Administration inquiry of the chemicals your employees handle).

If you find it difficult to formulate an appropriate program, do not hesitate to gather suggestions from your employees. They constantly watch things and people go in and out, and may have excellent suggestions for controlling that process. Also remember that your program must relate to the kind of people that you employ (of all the sources of leaks, employees present the greatest problems). It may be both necessary and appropriate to devise an elaborate set of precautions and rules to define clerical employees' appropriate behavior. However, too many restrictions can alienate the more professional, creative employee, and you may have to depend more heavily on employee education and motivation.

Manage the Program

Finally, after devoting the required time and effort to determine your needs and the best way to meet them, assign someone to be permanently responsible for the continous review and assessment of your Trade Secret Protection Program. This person will both enforce the program and evaluate its performance from time to time, adding or dropping features as required. This review function is essential.

Once you have established a program, you must stay with it. In fact, if any litigation occurs, your position will be worse if you have not followed your procedures than if you had never established them. If you find that

[1]If you *are* a licensee, you may be in breach of your contract if you don't take reasonable steps to protect the information you have acquired through license. This is especially true if you are using that information (or product) by passing it on to others. On the other hand, if you are a *licensor*, your plan must ensure that your licensees take the necessary steps to protect your trade secrets.

an aspect of your program is no longer useful, then eliminate it and document the change.

Both the system and the information it protects will periodically change. Therefore, you need procedures for *de*classifying, as well as classifying and protecting proprietary information. This can be effectively handled only through centralized control. If your organization is large enough, you may commit a full-time manager to the task. In smaller operations it may be one of several responsibilities given to a particular manager. In every case, it is critical to assign responsibility for continuous enforcement and review of your program.

The rest of this chapter treats the specifics of protection systems and provides a practical checklist. However, don't assume you must employ every measure to qualify your data for legal protection. At the same time, this list is not necessarily exhaustive. The specifics of your operations and the inventiveness of potential thieves make it impossible to describe every conceivable security technique. Nevertheless, these specific suggestions may provide several useful ideas to apply to your business.

Security Systems

Remember the double purpose of a protection system: to prevent theft, and to create an *image* of security that will move the judge or jury to give "after-the-fact" protection to your trade secrets. You may not regard a poster as an effective tool for stopping or even slowing down the employee who intends to steal confidential data. However, unrolling that same poster in court can have a dramatic impact on a jury.

Secure The Building

Consider first the physical layout of your facilities. Any areas containing your most valued confidential or proprietary information should be separated by locked doors, gates, and fences. Where possible, geographically separate facilities which store or use this information, such as research and development departments. And within those areas, provide appropriate storage, including locked filing and drawing cabinets. This makes it easier to enforce rules against casual treatment of documentation. You create an atmosphere that encourages careful use of these documents, and provide a ready means to care for them.

Pay particular attention to your receiving areas where non-employee activity frequently occurs and where a considerable amount of sensitive information can be found. Consider requiring vendors to ship raw materials or chemicals in plain, coded containers, with no indication of contents or suppliers. Indeed, some companies create "dummy" corporations at other facilities for the sole purpose of receiving their component materials in a secure fashion.

Determine the most critical areas of your facility, and limit access accordingly. Post signs prominently, to warn both employees and others that only authorized persons may enter. Enforce these limitations by using badges with the employee's photograph. Devise a color code for signs or posters (or even the building's interior decor) that reflects levels of the employee security clearance. This will make it easy for the employee to understand where he's supposed to be and easy to spot an employee who is in the wrong place. For extremely sensitive areas, consider using magnetically coded key-cards or other sophisticated locking systems.

Guard the Photocopier

The invention of the photocopier has to be one of the greatest boons to the industrial spy. In most facilities, several machines are located in rooms with easy access, but without easy surveillance. Often, extra copies are left in the wastebasket for cleaning crews or whoever else may happen by. In most decentralized copying systems, no controls specify what documents can be copied or how many copies can be made. Most companies consider the photocopier a cost control problem, but for many it is a greater security problem. If your security system is to have any integrity at all, you must create and enforce substantial controls on photocopier use. Centralize the location of copiers where possible and situate them in open areas to limit concealed activities. Provide shredders or other secure means of disposal near the copying area. Instruct employees on the limitations of copier use and post warning signs visible to someone using the machine. Of course, the most reliable security system completely centralizes the copying function, giving certain employees sole responsibility for receiving documents to be copied and for doing the work.

Control Visitors

Many courts consider visitor control the most telling factor in assessing the importance a company places on its confidential information. Permit only one entrance for visitors and control or monitor all other entrances. A receptionist should always be present to maintain a log for visitors and off-hour employees. The log book should be completely filled out by each visitor to include one's name, address, affiliation, reason for visit, person being seen at the facility, and times and dates of entering and leaving. The requirement to sign in and out must be strictly monitored and enforced. Require the receptionist to check all credentials of repair persons or others who might be left in areas of the facility without an escort.

Visitors who might be admitted to a secure area or otherwise be exposed to confidential information should sign a simple nondisclosure agreement *before* leaving the reception area. Here is a sample form:

Name (print) ______________________ Date ____________
Affiliation ____________________________________

In consideration of being admitted to the facilities of ____________ Corporation, I agree to uphold in the strictest confidence any proprietary information which is disclosed to me. I agree not to remove any document, equipment, or other materials from the premises, and that I will not photograph or otherwise record any information to which I may have access during my visit.

Visitor: ____________________________________

Escort: ____________________________________

Issue all visitors a badge or temporary insignia which plainly indicates whether an escort is required. Clearly define and consistently enforce your escort policy. Security personnel should be alert to visitors bearing the "escort" insignia who are unescorted within the facility. Arrange tours for limited areas of the building, and notify in advance security personnel and employees in the tour areas. Clearly mark areas which are off limits to any visitors. Finally, instruct and regularly remind all employees not to discuss company business or product information with any unescorted visitor.

Do not neglect the more "traditional" forms of security such as posted guards, electronic surveillance (television cameras), and physical intrusion systems. While these measures may not always deter the determined individual from carrying out sensitive information in a briefcase, it will profoundly impact the court or jury. Finally, consider regular "debugging" of offices, meeting rooms, and homes of key employees.

Interview Employees

Remember, employees constitute the most significant source of confidential information leaks. Therefore, a key part of your program will include methods for diminishing the risk of such leaks. In brief, you must hit employees hard coming and going. Impress upon the prospective or departing employee the importance you attach to your confidential information.

Entrance Interviews. An opportunity frequently missed is the pre-employment interview. Establish an understanding with a prospective employee regarding the importance of your proprietary information. Emphasize it is a valuable, expensive asset of the company which can be easily lost by negligent disclosure. You want the employee to come on board firmly committed to the idea that "loose lips sink ships."

Another objective of the interview is to weed out possible spies and to alert yourself to any weaknesses that might make the new employee particularly susceptible to espionage. Also, assure yourself that the new employee does not bring in anyone else's confidential information, so that the employment you are offering will not expose you to a potential lawsuit. By conducting such interviews, you will be making an excellent record of both your intent not to steal the trade secrets of any former employer and of your attempt to protect your own.

Consider two principles in conducting preemployment interviews: conduct them according to a standard procedure (use a checklist which will go into the employee's file), and always conduct them *before* the employee begins work.

Debrief. Begin the interview with a series of questions to the new employee. First, find out why the employee left his or her former employer. Exploring the causes of dissatisfaction often reveals any potential problem areas at a new job. Next, ask whether any special confidentiality obligations or restrictions (including any nondisclosure or invention agreements) existed with the former employer. The response will alert you to a potential claim by the former employer of your interference with those obligations. It may indicate isolating the employee from particular departments, or even terminating the relationship if the former employer's proprietary information would necessarily be compromised in the new position. (For example, the employee may be subject to an agreement which requires assigning to the former employer all inventions the employee conceives during a given period after termination of previous employment.)

You cannot make an informed, rational decision about the risk taken in hiring an individual until you have fully explored what types of proprietary data were involved in the previous job, especially if that job was with a major competitor. Moreover, this area of questioning often reveals the employee's attitude toward obligations of confidentiality. Those who exhibit an uncommitted or blasé attitude should be closely counseled and perhaps closely watched as well.

Learn the specific areas and projects the employee previously worked on. Determine whether any chance of improper use or disclosure of the former employer's trade secrets exists. Get the interviewee to be candid. Don't treat lightly the subject of the former employer's proprietary data, even if you both believe that none exists.

Find out if the employee received any warning or was asked to sign any nondisclosure documents when leaving the prior position. If the interview discloses any problems in this area, the appropriate management, and possibly company counsel, must become involved. It may be serious enough to warrant not hiring the person. As an alternative, you may arrange work in a non-sensitive position or area for a period of time, or decide that the risk is low enough to require no extraordinary steps. Whatever the outcome, your decision will be an informed one and you will have created a further record of your good intentions that may serve you well in any later litigation.

Educate. In addition to asking questions, use the preemployment interview as a counseling session. Be sure that the prospective employee completely understands what the company regards as proprietary information. The security program must be discussed as a "real" topic. Do not simply throw forms, handbooks, and memoranda at the interviewee for later review. Answer all questions regarding employee obligations and the security program. Provide a name of someone within the company to whom the employee can address future questions about confidential information and his or her duties to protect it from unauthorized use.

Finally, before completing the interview, ask the new employee to review and sign a nondisclosure agreement. This document can take many forms, and is discussed later in this chapter. It may include agreements assigning inventions, restricting competition, and the like. Minimally, however, it must consist of the employee's promise to hold in confidence the company's proprietary information and not to use or disclose it in any way that is inconsistent with employment in the company. Explain the seriousness of this document and make sure it is understood. Be certain that the employee reads the document completely, has all questions answered, and signs it before beginning work.

Exit Interviews. The goals and opportunities of interviews given the departing employees are

- Leave them with the impression that they have a firm obligation to you which you will enforce if necessary (mental attitudes are extremely important, since the information you seek to protect may be carried in the employee's head).
- To prevent the pilferage or improper use of your proprietary information (an employee who experiences a well-planned, thorough exit interview is unlikely to take any sensitive information).
- To demonstrate the importance of protecting your trade secrets to other employees, the outside world, and to a judge or jury.
- To gather information about your competition.
- To find out why the employee is leaving. This information may reveal significant problems with your operations, and you may be able to prevent others from leaving for the same reasons. At the minimum, you will be able to evaluate more intelligently the risk of losing your trade secrets.

Like the entrance interview, the exit interview must be characterized by an unwavering procedure, ideally using a form or checklist. It may be conducted by the personnel or security departments or by either one in conjunction with the employee's manager. However, it must be performed by someone trained in the process, and who exercises excellent judgment.

Preliminary Research. Before the interview begins, check appropriate records to verify that the employee has turned in all information, equipment, and materials that have been checked out, or which you would otherwise assume the employee to possess (for example, engineering notebooks, business plans, progress reports, marketing plans and studies, customer lists, and so on).

Check with the employee's supervisors to learn of any recent unusual activity, such as using photocopiers excessively, taking documents from the premises, or doing substantial work at home. Whenever possible, prepare a list of the specific trade secrets which have been exposed during employment, to review during the interview. With all of this to consider, you will need time to prepare for the interview. However, be ready to conduct the procedure on a moment's notice, since it is common practice for departing employees with extremely sensitive positions to be ushered immediately from the building after giving notice or being terminated.

Debrief and Reeducate. Also, as in the entrance interview, be prepared to ask predetermined questions and make predetermined statements. If the employee refuses to answer any of the questions, don't press the matter, but note the refusal and any reasons given for it on the interview form. Try to find out where the employee will be working and about his or her new responsibilities. Get as many specifics as possible. Determine how the new job was offered, and why the decision to leave was made. Discuss this subject in depth to learn whether others plan to leave for similar reasons, so you can take appropriate protective measures.

Explore the employee's understanding of the sensitive information involved in his or her duties, and the meaning of the nondisclosure obligations. If that discussion reveals a poor attitude, be particularly careful in dealing with the employee and be emphatic about those obligations. Find out whether any work was performed at home, and what materials or equipment may be there (including notebooks, company publications, or anything else related to the company). Make arrangements for picking up all company materials.

Don't read from a prepared text (as opposed to a checklist or notes). It is simply not convincing. Also, avoid any "inquisition" or an unnecessarily threatening tone. You may need this employee's help at a later time (perhaps as a consultant, or to assist in prosecuting a patent application, or simply to explain some of the work left behind). Nevertheless, be firm enough to leave the unmistakable impression that the employee has serious commitments to you, which continue after the termination of employment.

Caution the employee against taking, using, or disclosing any of the company's proprietary information. Be as specific as possible, but don't pretend to be all-inclusive. Express it in terms such as, "as you know, our trade secrets and confidential information *include* the following." In general, emphasize two points. First, your trade secrets are real, and they are valuable company assets. Second, the employee has a special duty, by virtue of employment, to protect—forever—the confidentiality of that information (and you will go after any employee who fails in that duty).

Explain that company trade secrets need not be expressed in a document and may exist only in the employee's head; that does not make them any less the company's property nor does it lessen the employee's obligation to protect them from unauthorized use. Many employees desire to take work samples, or consider those little black books of customer names and addresses as personal property. Explain that such materials belong to you and must be returned. Provide a copy of the nondisclosure agreement that the employee signed at the beginning of employment. Finally, request the employee to sign a "termination statement," adapted from the following form (remember that a refusal to sign such a statement, like a refusal to give information at the exit interview, may itself be useful in any later litigation, to demonstrate an evil motive on the part of the employee).

Termination Statement

I hereby certify that I do not have in my possession, nor have I failed to return, any notebooks, drawings, notes, reports, proposals, or other documents or materials (or copies or extracts thereof) or tools, equipment, or other property belonging to ______________ Corporation.

I also certify that I have complied with and will continue to comply with all of the provisions of the Agreement regarding proprietary information which I have previously signed, including my obligation to preserve as confidential all proprietary, technical, and business information pertaining to ______________ Corporation.

Before the employee leaves, supervise the cleaning of desk and office areas, and the return of any keys, cards, and the like. For especially sensitive employees, or those with substantial knowledge on critical subjects, consider a formal "debriefing" session. This will provide continuity to the remaining staff and flush out any potential problems requiring immediate attention. If the interview process reveals that others may be leaving, consider meeting with the employee's co-workers and supervisors, to gather appropriate information, find solutions to keep your staff, and impress them with the seriousness of the situation. Again, avoid overreacting and creating a "witch hunt" atmosphere. Finally, write a follow-up letter, summarizing the employee's obligations. And consider sending a cautionary letter to the new employer. Suggested forms for both of these letters appear in the Appendices B and C.

Control Documents

The most sensitive and important trade secrets are documented. Controlling those documents is a critical part of your security system. And because multiple documents circulate throughout the modern business environment, the integrity of the design and enforcement of document control becomes paramount. Carefully establish this subsystem, regularly review it, and religiously enforce it. Consider whether to let employees take work home. If you allow it, create procedures for identifying the materials removed, ensuring their proper use, protection, and return. Enforcing this policy requires effort, but it can be done. However, if enforcement becomes lax or ineffective, then the procedure must be scrapped or modified to reflect reality. If it is proved in court that you have not followed your document control system, it may be worse than if you had never created it at all.

Develop Procedures

Begin designing your system by studying the generation, circulation, storage, and disposal of your documents. Consider your present situation in light of the suggestions which follow to define your critical problem areas.

Document generation presents the most obvious and perhaps easiest area of control. First, establish procedures and standards for identifying documents that require protection from disclosure or improper use. Consider establishing different levels of confidentiality.

Minimally, however, you must define and publish for all employees exactly what types of documents must be protected (for suggested specifics, see Appendix D). Clearly indicate on the front of all documents any applicable confidentiality restrictions. Print such a legend on regularly used forms (for example, proposals, drawings, title pages, and so on). For other documents use a rubber stamp. The notice should state the document is your property, and delineate any restrictions on its use. Some examples include the following:

- "This document contains proprietary information belonging to Corporation, and its receipt of possession does not convey any rights to reproduce, disclose its contents, or to manufacture, use or sell anything it may describe. Reproduction, disclosure, or use without specific written authorization of Corporation is strictly forbidden."

- "This is a confidential document with controlled distribution. Copies may only be made through department XYZ [security]."
- "COMPANY CONFIDENTIAL — DO NOT COPY."

Documents submitted to a government agency may be subject to inspection and copying under the Freedom of Information Act. Certain exemptions from disclosure are listed in the statute, at Title 4, Section 552 of the U.S. Code. Clearly mark your confidential documents as "confidential trade secrets" and indicate the subsection(s) under which you claim an exemption. Although this will not guarantee nondisclosure to third parties, it may prevent inadvertent disclosure, and enhances the overall strength of your security program.

When confidential documents must be handled by several employees, many of whom are not well-educated, consider devising a color-coded system to reflect levels of confidentiality. Such procedures should complement, and not replace, the normal legends. For documents that require wide circulation, use envelopes with appropriate cautionary phrases printed on the outside. To restrict photocopying of extremely sensitive documents, issue colorful tags for each "original" in circulation. Permanently affix the tag to the front of the document. Any copy found without a tag or with a photoprint of the tag would presumptively be unauthorized. Consider reproducing the document on paper with color coded "confidential" markings. Unauthorized photocopies would be black and white.

Another useful technique for tracking multiple copies of an extremely sensitive document (such as a business plan) requires numbering each individual copy, maintaining a log of the individuals receiving each copy, and recording check-out and return times. This procedure can include a form signed by recipients whereby they promise not to pass it on or copy it and to return it on demand. With this system, a quick glance at the log book would indicate how many copies are in circulation and where each one is located.

"Public" Information. New documents that address outsiders require special screening. This includes promotional literature such as brochures, advertisements, press releases, and material dispersed at trade shows, which should be subject to prior review. Trade shows present a particularly dangerous problem, since the proximity of the competition permits easy access to a wealth of free information.

Devise a procedure for reviewing articles and books written by employees for publication. The employee's goal of professional prestige is inherently inconsistent with maintaining the secrecy of your information. Therefore, monitor this area closely.

Finally, examine handbooks and repair manuals provided to customers. These should prominently display confidentiality legends, especially on drawings; don't depend solely on a copyright notice. In preparing these materials, never disclose more information than necessary. Secure an acknowledgment from the customer that the manual remains your property and is "loaned" for use with your product. If you use the "loan" technique, however, be sure you establish and follow a procedure to ensure proper return.

Private Information. Other problem areas related to document generation include: internal marketing documents (remember, sales representatives only feel comfortable when they are talking), financial documents, drawings and blueprints, and specifications and proposals. On each page of computer program listings note the information is "_____ Corporation-Confidential." Require engineering notebooks to be permanently bound and titled. Clearly display the employee and company name, confidentiality legend, and a statement of company ownership. The notebooks should provide space for witness signatures and dates. At the outset, instruct employees on how to use these notebooks. Enforce a procedure for controlling and retrieving them at termination of employment.

Circulate confidential documents only to those with a "need to know." If you have no system, procedures, or standards for determining who needs access to particular documents, then any circulation control system will be meaningless and you will have put another nail in the coffin of your trade secret case. Just establishing those procedures is not sufficient; you must also design appropriate controls to guarantee those documents are properly circulated. This involves many of the methods already discussed in this section. In addition, your internally published procedures should include instructions for storing and using documents to ensure that the information they contain is not made available to anyone—within or without the company—who does not have a need to know.

Disposal and Reclassification. Finally, develop a program for disposal of confidential documents. Regularly review the inventory of controlled documentation, and declassify information no longer deemed confidential. If you simply classify all documents confidential and never remove the restriction, or never establish a procedure for declassification, the integrity of your claim of confidentiality for *all* of your information may be questioned. Find a safe method to dispose of these and any other unneeded copies. Do not throw them away. Shred or otherwise destroy such documents on the premises. Be sure sufficient facilities are available to do this.

Protect Information Processing Systems

In the past 20 years, we have witnessed astonishing developments in the use of computers. The computing power which used to cost half a million dollars and fill a room now costs only a few dollars and fits on a chip smaller than your thumbnail. The invention of the microprocessor has permitted the wide-scale use of data processing in the most mundane office environment. While electronic data communication and storage may not entirely replace paper, it will dramatically increase the amount of raw data that the average business can store, retrieve, and manipulate.

The implications of this development for the protection of your trade secrets are significant. The processing power now at your command can increase your ability to pursue technological advances in your field, and enable you to compete more effectively in the marketplace and produce a better product or service. Computer technology fundamentally affects your ability to develop your "intellectual property" assets. By using electric typewriters, office minicomputers, electronic mail, and inter-office computer networks, you can rapidly produce competitively sensitive business information, such as market analyses, marketing plans, and financial information.

The trouble is, when something explodes it becomes difficult to contain. You are participating in an information explosion which can provide enormous benefits to your business. At the same time, it presents an equally enormous challenge. First, the amount of information which needs protection has vastly increased. Second, methods of information production and storage permit accessibility by more people. Third, providing security for this data requires different and more complex procedures. Broken locks and other evidence of physical intrusion may alert you to the compromised security of your stored documents. But when highly skilled thieves gain access to electronically stored data, it is far more difficult even to learn of the intrusion.

No single system protects all computer-stored information. The type and degree of protection depends on circumstances of your business. Consider the kind of computer system you use, and the level of confidentiality it supports. Is it a "stand-alone" office computer, or an inter-office communications network with several work stations sharing the same computer? Or is it a remote or timeshare computing system, where your data is stored several hundred miles away on a large computer, along with the data of many other companies?

Also consider the type of information you store. As the technology of electronic data processing surges ahead, new security techniques will be developed to assist in the fight against "computer crime." Nevertheless, several points are worth considering, regardless of the nature and extent of your involvement with computers.

Control Data Access and Integrity

Considering your dual goals of establishing security and the appearance of security, your first concern in protecting computer-stored trade secrets is access. Control and supervise access to terminals. Regularly modify user names and passwords, especially where you experience high employee turnover. Assign someone to regularly monitor system access and usage under particular user names and to periodically review transactions to spot any abnormalities.

For especially high levels of security, consider encrypting your data. This essentially scrambles the computer language according to a separate, complex computer program. Unless you have the code, you simply cannot understand or use the data. In the past, such systems have been quite expensive, since encoded material requires significantly greater storage. However, advances in technology *may* decrease the cost of storage enough to support encryption as a cost-effective technique in a wider range of applications.

When you store data electronically, you must not only consider theft, but also potential loss through human error or a system malfunction. Therefore, it is imperative to maintain "archival" copies of the data files manipulated on the system.

Many experts firmly believe the secure computer system does not exist. Given the rapidly changing technology and the easy access to most computer systems, that is not a surprising conclusion. With enough time, a sufficiently intelligent person could break into most data banks. The news media seem to delight in reporting events like the bank teller who transfers millions of dollars into a personal account without detection, or the high school senior who manages to gain access to a school's computerized attendance records. However, we cannot expect absolute security from *any* system, short of Fort Knox; and it is unlikely that you are willing to spend that kind of money. Rather, you must employ a system that will make it reasonably difficult for the prospective thief to steal your trade secrets. This is certainly possible to achieve without extraordinary cost, using present technology.

You must also employ the more "theatrical" measures to convince the outside world, your employees, and any future court of your determination to protect these assets, and to make it highly unpleasant for anyone who breaches your security. In that respect, protecting electronically stored information is no different than protecting any other form of proprietary information.

Maintain Records And Perform Audits

Chapter 1 discussed the importance of analyzing the type and amount of proprietary information you need to protect, in order to determine what type and amount of protection you require. But, you cannot know how well your protection system works unless you regularly review it. The success of a security system depends on enforcing the system. It is a sad and difficult lesson if you learn in litigation that the enforcement of your system has been overly lax.

Record the Users

Starting again at the beginning, *identify* all proprietary information, by category, item, and location. Maintain a list or log identifying your confidential technology and business information. Require each department manager to produce and update lists to be incorporated into the master list, and assign one person to collect and maintain this information. This record will prove useful to remind a departing employee of specific things which require continued confidentiality, or avoid an expensive lawsuit by convincing a competitor's lawyer in advance of your documented case. It will also help when, simply through the cataloging process, you discover additional information which requires protection. The process of creating these lists, then, must be a continuous one, with periodic updating by responsible managers.

Record who has access to each trade secret, or class of trade secrets. This process may reveal people who are on distribution lists or who otherwise have access to data who do not have a need to know. Indeed, when you first create this list you may be shocked at the broad distribution of highly sensitive documents.

Take corrective action to restrict access to your most sensitive information to the fewest people possible. In the event of a security breach, your records would readily provide a list of personnel to interview, both to determine how the breach occurred and how best to prevent its recurrence. For specific, highly sensitive documents, such as business plans or marketing plans, always maintain a log listing each person receiving a copy, the inventory number of the copy received, and the dates of its distribution and return. Employ this procedure with the most critical information to track leaks, and enhance your position in winning or avoiding litigation.

Audit the System

A security system audit proves useful in several situations. For instance, if your proprietary information is included in submissions to the government, you may need to review your procedures and establish a means of classifying and identifying such submissions, enabling them to survive a request for disclosure under the Freedom of Information Act. Also, if your contracts require the return of your documentation upon the termination of a relationship, be sure to institute effective retrieval procedures. In one case, the court denied trade secret protection primarily because the owner failed to recover documentation which had been properly disclosed to an outsider.

Audit procedures must include *destruction* as well as protection. To avoid cluttering files with old information, and to ensure your system receives proper "respect" in court, be sure to devote as much attention to declassify and remove information from the system as you did to identify and protect it. Moreover, though certain documents are no longer useful to you, and ought to be declassified, the information may remain useful to a competitor who might learn what technology you have rejected or how you make business decisions. Therefore, your audit must also analyze how effectively you destroy your records, to guarantee against recirculating this information.

Finally, your audit system should include procedures for detecting thefts of your proprietary information. Consider first your own employees whose properly guided loyalty will encourage them to report suspicious circumstances in or out of the facility. Sales representatives regularly discuss competing products with other sales representatives and customers. They may be the first to know when your competitor announces a product unusually close to yours, or which took an unusually brief time to develop. Moreover, they regularly attend trade shows, conferences, and the like. While warning them not to discuss the company's confidential data, encourage them to listen to others. Not only will they gain general information about the competition, but they may also discover information indicating improper use of your intellectual property.

There are many other examples. Your purchasing department may learn that a competitor has requested your vendors and suppliers to produce goods or services related to your trade secret. Indeed, they may have been provided with designs, drawings, or samples identical to yours. Alert employees who attend industry conferences, hear technical presentations or review technical publications to the use of your proprietary data or drawings. Personnel working with your printers may learn that a competitor has attempted to use the printer as a source for discovering your trade secrets. Even the personnel department can assist, by monitoring the help wanted ads placed by competitors attempting to hire away key employees working on particularly sensitive projects.

Chapter 4 covers how to proceed after you discover a competitor is using your trade secrets. This includes the circumstance of the terminated employee who joins the competition or begins an independent competitive business.

However, what do you do if you discover that one of your present employees has violated obligations of confidence? First, gather as much information as you can *before* confronting the employee. Through discreet investigation and a thorough review of your records, determine what trade secret information was accessible to the employee, whether the employee gained irregular access to information, and whether the employee has exhibited any unusual behavior such as excessive copying of documents, removal of documents or equipment from the premises, or working at odd hours. As discreetly as possible, investigate whether the information has been disclosed to anyone outside the company, and if so, to whom. After gathering this information conduct a conference with the employee. In as non-threatening a manner as possible, determine whether any legitimate explanation exists for the unusual activity and whether there has, in fact, been a breach of security.

Focus on discovering where the information has gone rather than on punishing the employee. This is not your normal employee theft situation. Your primary concern is retrieving the property, since it may lose its value entirely if disseminated too widely. Once you have secured all of the information possible, contact your counsel immediately to determine whether you should terminate the employee and how to proceed. (You may incur liability for defamation if you cannot show cause and the employee cannot obtain other employment, because of the termination.) Counsel will advise whether to refer the matter to the district attorney and to determine how to retrieve your proprietary information and to protect it from further disclosure.

Employee Relations

Employees are your single greatest resource and your single greatest expense. As we have just reviewed, employees can play a significant role in protecting your trade secrets. However, they are also the single greatest cause of lost confidential information, most often through simple ignorance or inadvertence. Therefore, create systems which make it difficult for employees to make mistakes. You must foster an attitude that trade secrets are important and that all employees must conscientiously protect them from improper disclosure.

Establish Employee Procedures

Develop that attitude by creating policies and procedures which outline every employee's responsibilities for protecting your trade secrets. After such direction, the employees will be less likely to compromise your confidential information, whether inadvertently or not. In litigation concerning an employee or an employee's role in protecting your trade secrets, these policy statements will positively demonstrate the employee's knowledge of your trade secrets and the responsibilities assigned to protect against their improper disclosure.

Be cautious in this area, however. Once you have established employee procedures, you must follow them to the letter. Failure to do so may be worse than not having established the procedures at all. For example, if a particular marketing document has been made available to persons in several departments, or to a limited number of persons outside the company, a case can still be made that disclosure was not so broad as to defeat trade secret status. However, the case will be harder to establish if your policy restricted the document's distribution to the marketing department.

Appendix D provides a sample "Policy Manual" for employees. Whether published separately, or included in an employee handbook, you must provide a policy statement to current employees as soon as possible, and to all new employees before they begin work. Require the personnel department to regularly distribute the policy statement during the initiation procedure. Consider requiring employees to acknowledge in writing their receipt and understanding of the policies. Conduct question-answer sessions to inform new employees and to remind and update previously hired employees. This area of employee education will be addressed more completely later in this chapter.

Although your particular needs will determine the policies you adopt, consider the following:

- Divide the knowledge of your trade secrets among several individuals. The temptation to improperly use part of a secret is not as great, and a partial disclosure may be meaningless. It also makes it more difficult for your employees to leave and compete with you by using your trade secrets and helps protect against successful "raiding" by a competitor who might otherwise try to hire away key employees simply to gain access to your trade secrets.

- Disseminate proprietary or confidential information only through established channels. Strictly controlled publication protects against unauthorized disclosure, and will help demonstrate in litigation that any leak was unauthorized and improper. Finally, it helps coordinate disclosures among company departments that may have conflicting objectives, and brings those conflicts to the surface before they become problems.

- Consider to what extent you should define your trade secrets for employees. As the Motorola case demonstrated, you are taking a substantial risk if you simply tell your employees "we have trade secrets" and wait until litigation to define them. Also, as previously described, several excellent independent reasons support analyzing and cataloging your proprietary and confidential data.

  At the same time, you cannot provide a widely circulated definition that reveals the substance of your trade secrets. Nor should you give the impression that your list is exhaustive. You may develop new trade secrets after the employee receives the information and before you have provided an update. Therefore, define your trade secrets in a *general* fashion, providing appropriate examples, and qualifying that your "list" is not all-inclusive.

Supplement this information with periodic departmental meetings to advise employees of information which is particularly relevant to their group. (If you do conduct such sessions, be sure to maintain a record of who attended and what was said.)

- Define who has access to particularly sensitive areas of your facility and under what conditions. This not only deters certain employees from entering off-limits areas, but alerts them to the presence of unauthorized individuals within a given area.

- Define the document protection and control system, and indicate the employee's responsibilities within that system.

- Require prior review of an employee's technical speeches and publications. The employee whose professional standing and ego satisfaction are in direct conflict with your desire to maintain secrecy cannot be expected to properly determine what can be publicly disclosed. Properly described and delicately enforced, this procedure should not be perceived as a threat to academic independence or First Amendment rights.

- Require some level of management review of any third party nondisclosure agreement an employee signs on behalf of the company. Mid- to lower-level employees often negotiate license agreements, for example. In that situation, the prospective licensor often presents a nondisclosure agreement (for an example, see Appendix E). These agreements are entirely proper, and aid in evaluating a proposed license or purchase of a product or technology. However, without some independent review, it is possible that the obligations undertaken in these documents could unintentionally interfere with the present operations or future research work of the company. It could prohibit the company from employing technology it already has or could independently develop.

- Establish a policy regarding removing company property from the premises and for doing work at home with company documents.

Educate to Prevent Disclosure

Most secrets are lost through employee inadvertence. Telling your employees what they need to do will increase your chances of protecting your confidential information. Your educational program will assist in trade secret litigation. It demonstrates that you consider your proprietary information to be worth the effort, and documents the individual employee's awareness of the need to protect the information. Primarily, however, employee education prevents disclosure.

Employee education in the trade secret area, like safety, must be continuous and not simply the focus of a single meeting or campaign prompted by an unpleasant experience. The effects of a one-shot effort can quickly wear off, while repetition reinforces the importance of the subject matter. In addition, both your employees and your trade secrets change over time. Periodically define your intellectual property and review your protection measures with those who realistically control them.

In developing an educational program, focus on informing each employee:

- What comprises your proprietary technology and confidential business information.
- How seriously you intend to protect it.
- What particular obligations within the total protection system that employee must accept.

Within the boundaries these objectives describe, your program will reflect the amount and type of confidential information you need to protect, the number of employees, the extent to which your employees have access to your confidential information and costs.

The entrance interview was introduced as a particularly opportune time for beginning the educational process. In addition, continue to disseminate this information throughout employment through a handbook (see Appendix D), circulars, articles in the employee newsletter, signs, and posters. Employee conferences and meetings provide a special opportunity for dialogue in this often misunderstood area. Larger companies might hold separate meetings with managers who then conduct department sessions, focusing on the specific information they need to protect and describing their own security measures.

Develop special techniques for training your sales force. For some reason, many sales representatives don't control their tongues. Often they receive anonymous inquiries from "potential customers" requesting information about a product "in order to understand its possible applications." These situations present potential information leaks; one can pick up significant details from what sales personnel offer as simply "collateral" information. Train your sales and customer support personnel to know what can and cannot be said.

Better yet, restrict their *access* to what cannot be said. Keep them away from designers and engineers, and do not permit engineers to respond to customer inquiries. Finally, when developing your special "course" for sales personnel, examine in detail and with great emphasis the trade show or convention. Such events are a dangerous marketing practice, since they invite extensive socializing among industry competitors, threatening trade secret preservation.

Your employees provide an excellent source of information on events and situations within your facilities. While no one enjoys or condones open solicitation of snitches, you can take positive steps to increase the effectiveness of employee feedback. First, provide special training to employees in superior positions to observe security breaches, such as receptionists, freight loaders, copy machine operators, and the like. Second, when special circumstances raise concern assign "spies" to observe particular people or areas within the plant.

Create Supportive Incentives

Various approaches for preserving your proprietary information have been discussed. Now let's examine how to develop more information. Again, your employees play the largest role here; apart from your purchase or license of technology, employees are the primary producers of proprietary information.

Cash awards encourage invention and innovation among employees. The prospect of receiving money both encourages creativity and provides motivation not to steal the final product. However, some significant problems accompany this approach. If you establish a program to pay employees the cash "value" of their inventions, ideas, or suggestions, you invite the problem of valuation. Trying to determine how much money a particular process or invention has saved the company can be an accounting nightmare; and it can result in a far larger award to the employee than you intended.

Promising a percentage of the income realized from sales or licensing of employee inventions may improve the accounting situation, but may also create an implied duty of the company (a duty which is difficult to avoid, even by contract) to exploit the invention for maximum dollar return. Even if you establish a company committee to determine an appropriate amount, or award a "flat fee" prize, it implies that you are paying the employee in return for a benefit. When the employee feels that the payment received was not commensurate with the benefit provided, a suit might follow. Lockheed dramatically learned this lesson in June 1981 when a California jury returned a verdict against it of $2.5 million (including punitive damages) for failure to pay two employees the full value of inventions produced under a monetary incentive plan.

If you decide that the possible pitfalls of cash incentives outweigh the potential benefits, all is not lost. An employee's incentive to invent may develop from a hope for personal glory, intellectual curiosity, and perhaps the desire to advance the interests of the company, or of the industry. Therefore, when one of your employees does invent, play it up. See that the employee's name and photograph are posted and published, and that the president or some other officer extends a dinner invitation. When a patent is issued in the employee's name, present an appropriate memento of the occasion, preferably in the presence of fellow workers.

Use your imagination. Sales representatives have regularly been spurred on to greater efforts by non-monetary incentives and the approach should apply as well to those who produce intellectual property.

Consider releasing an invention or concept to the employee when the company has decided not to use it after a specified time. This practice is widespread in Europe and indeed is enforced by national statutes. General Electric's program assisted its employees with funding for start-up ventures exploiting the invention (with equity participation by the company). Rather than buy itself a lawsuit, the company may have created a new and profitable business partner. It may not work in every case or in every industry, but it is certainly an approach to consider.

Agreements And Contracts

Contracts are central to trade secrets. They protect secrets by confirming obligations not to disclose information and they permit and stipulate use of the secret by other parties you choose to share it with. Written contracts are not always required. In many cases, the law will imply an obligation on the part of the person receiving the trade secret not to use it except for certain purposes, and not to disclose it. However, you will benefit from writing contracts rather than depending on the existence of such implied obligations, which can be difficult to prove. A final, general point to remember: Get contracts signed at the beginning of the relationship, or on the first occasion the other party gains access to your trade secrets.

Employees

A century ago, most innovation and invention occurred through the efforts of independent, individual inventors. Today, perhaps because of the high cost of innovation in a world of such complex technology, it is the *employed* inventor who is more likely to produce innovation. Generally speaking, the law implies an obligation on the part of each employee not to disclose the employer's trade secrets and imposes special obligations on a company's managers and officers.

Nondisclosure. Then why use contracts with employees? There are several good reasons. You may already use patent assignment agreements with several of your employees anyway, and you can easily add a nondisclosure provision. Also, signing a contract admitting the existence of your trade secrets deters the employee from later claiming that you have none. Employees are less likely to compromise confidential information when they know how seriously the company regards the subject. And considering the high turnover work force, a departing employee's new employer is less likely to cause or encourage the employee to violate secrecy obligations. Indeed, some extremely cautious employers may simply refuse to hire the employee or may avoid doing business in a particular area just to avoid litigation over a strongly worded contract. In practice, a court is more likely to give preventive relief against disclosure or use of trade secrets by a departing employee when the obligations have been spelled out clearly in a document. Finally, depending on the law of your state, you may gain protection the law does not imply through a contract (for example, a covenant not to compete after termination of employment).

Who should sign nondisclosure agreements? Everyone who might possibly have access to your trade secrets. Do not limit these agreements to engineers or other inventors who also sign patent assignment agreements. Many valuable trade secrets are produced and controlled by employees in other areas, such as marketing and production. However, consider using different agreements for different employees, depending on the degree and frequency of their access to trade secret material. (For example, there is no reason to have your clerical staff sign an agreement requiring advance review of published technical papers.) On the other hand, one agreement may suffice in a smaller business where fewer employees have more knowledge of and access to trade secrets.

The contract should be signed at the beginning of the employment relationship. In fact, provide a copy of the agreement to the prospective employee to review and sign before starting the job. This will eliminate the question of whether or not the agreement was signed voluntarily and whether adequate consideration was given in return for the promise. If you have not previously used such agreements, and now request your employees to sign them, the contracts may later be attacked since no new consideration was provided on signing. However, most states now permit these agreements to stand, reasoning that the offer of continued employment is sufficient consideration for the employee's promise. If you ask employees to sign an agreement at termination, you should offer something else, such as money. It would normally be a nominal amount and many companies only pay a discretionary severance allowance on the signing of such a document.

You may experience problems in requesting established employees to sign nondisclosure agreements. Many of those who have been with the company a long time and have provided good service will consider the document as a loyalty oath, and the request to sign it an insult. Since an employee nondisclosure agreement is not absolutely necessary, it is not worth losing good employees over the issue. However, add a memorandum to the personnel file of each employee who is not asked (or who refuses) to sign a nondisclosure covenant, indicating the reason for the exception. Provide the employee with a note (maintaining a copy in the file) confirming that, in view of the length of service, signing the document will not be required, though it only reflects the obligations that the law would impose.

A sample Proprietary Information and Invention Agreement including a nondisclosure clause appears in Appendix F. Use this form to develop your own employee contracts. Although appropriate for most applications in California in 1982, this form should not be used without reviewing the matter with your lawyer. In drafting an agreement, consider the following competing policy considerations which operate in this area:

- The right of employees to move about freely and secure employment for which they are trained.
- The right of the employer to protect information which belongs to it.
- The interest of the public in a free marketplace of work and ideas.

The court will apply these principles to decide whether to grant an injunction against an employee's working for a particular competitor.

Therefore, resist the temptation to draft your agreement in draconian terms, giving every conceivable advantage to the employer and none to the employee. The court's negative reaction to such a document may affect decisions on how to enforce the agreement.

Especially with lower-level employees, a "Christmas tree" approach to include every form of restraint may indicate overreaching by the employer and result in a failure to secure any enforcement. Indeed, many courts have stated that the cumulative effect of many "partial" legal restraints may be a "total restraint" on an employee, which is illegal.

Keep your agreement short and simple. The "plain English" movement in the legal field has taught many lawyers that straightforward prose is not only easier to understand but also easier to enforce than the drawn-out language they believe they are supposed to use.

Because the nondisclosure agreement is a permanent document, do not define in detail what you consider to be the company's trade secrets. Leave that matter for the employee handbook or other publication, as suggested earlier. Your inventory of trade secrets changes over time and you will require the flexibility to include any new developments in the employee's nondisclosure obligations. Therefore, the definition of your proprietary information should be broad enough to cover all proprietary technology and business information which you have developed or reasonably expect to develop, whether or not you actually use it.

In another provision, the agreement should recognize the validity of the company's policies and procedures, and require the employee to abide by them. This should include whatever changes may occasionally be made in those policies or procedures. This provision permits you to include less detail in the agreement concerning the employee's specific duties on controlling proprietary information.

Noncompetition Covenants. You may also protect your proprietary information through employment agreements by restricting the employee's competitive activities. There is normally no problem in enforcing an agreement not to engage in competitive activity (including organizational efforts) while the employee remains on your payroll. The problems arise in enforcing restrictions against competition *after* employment. Consider the general antipathy shown by the courts to restrictions on employee mobility. As a warning, seek the advice of counsel before attempting to enforce or even use these contracts.

A sample form of a noncompetition covenant appears in Appendix G. In some states, most notably California and Michigan, such contracts are unenforceable by statute, except in certain narrow circumstances (such as when they are given by a stockholder or proprietor in conjunction with the purchase of the business). Even where such agreements are recognized however, they must be "reasonable" in their geographic coverage, duration, and scope of work. In many states, the courts will apply a "blue pencil rule" to restrict the application of a noncompetition agreement to a smaller area and shorter period, and as restricted, enforce it.

In an effort to avoid obeying rules established for noncompetition agreements, some employers qualify certain post-employment benefits for employees who do not compete, or require forfeiture of benefits if an employee does compete. Use such provisions with extreme caution, since many courts have held them invalid as unreasonable restraints. In addition, any efforts on your part to restrain competition may reflect monopolistic or predatory practices which the antitrust laws prohibit; under certain circumstances, you could risk not only the unenforceability of the agreement but significant exposure for antitrust claims as well.

Nevertheless, there is generally no prohibition against an employee's agreement not to take future employment which would inherently require using or divulging the present employer's trade secrets. Although such a provision may be difficult to enforce, and although it may not provide the employer with anything beyond the employee's legally implied obligations, it may cause employees to think twice before signing with a direct competitor.

Rather than write a noncompetition clause into the employment agreement, you may negotiate with a departing "key" employee for a consulting agreement. In continuing the relationship for a period of time, you gain the opportunity to prohibit competitive activities with limited risk. Such an agreement must provide compensation commensurate with the effort required. Also, in drafting the noncompetition provision in the consulting agreement, restrict the consultant only as required to protect yourself. The part-time consulting agreement could be voided if it unreasonably prevents the consultant from working in a chosen field.

Employee to Consultant. At the beginning of the employment relationship consider entering into a consulting agreement, which will become effective upon termination. The employee agrees to remain available to the company as a consultant for a specified time after terminating regular employment. Again, you must pay a significant portion (perhaps half) of the employee's normal salary, and the consulting period should be reasonably short. In return for such payment, the employer may successfully prevent competition by the employee during the most critical period of a competing start-up venture. At least, it would substantially minimize the impact of the otherwise sudden departure of a key employee.

Consultants

Because they have many of the privileges of a regular employee, though for a shorter period of time, consultants must be subject to nondisclosure obligations as well. Indeed, it is essential to secure such agreements from consultants; the nature of their work suggests they will work for a competitor, or may compete with you directly. (For a suggested form of agreement, see Appendix H.)

Vendors

Include the following language, or something similar, on all purchase orders and purchase agreements:

> "Vendor agrees to maintain in confidence all information provided in connection with this order and to use such information only for purposes of filling this order. Upon termination of work, all documents containing such information shall be returned to vendee."

In addition to the usual legends and stamps you use to distinguish your proprietary information, and to the provisions in your vendor agreements for protecting your proprietary information, use the following legend (or something similar) on any document you provide to your vendors:

> "This document contains data which is proprietary to Corporation and is provided only for limited use in filling its purchase order. This data may not be otherwise used or disclosed. This legend shall appear on any copy or extract made of this document."

In addition to vendors who sell goods, consider service vendors who regularly visit company facilities (for example, cleaning crews, equipment repair personnel). Secure a basic nondisclosure agreement from such vendors, especially if you do not regularly require all non-employee visitors to sign such a document.

Customers and Sales Agents

Sales agents, like employed sales personnel, are potentially significant sources of leaks. Inform them of what they can and cannot disclose, and always subject them to a written nondisclosure agreement. Unlike the employee, the sales agent's position is not so clearly confidential and requires the clearer definition a contract offers.

In dealing with customers, the contract is the *only* way to protect your trade secrets. Even if your technology could be discovered by "reverse-engineering" the product, a strongly worded confidentiality agreement will temper the customer's temptation to perform the process.

In some circumstances, you may be required to secure appropriate guarantees of confidentiality from your customers. For example, if the product includes confidential information acquired under license from a third party, you would be in breach of the license agreement if you didn't secure such guarantees. Always include these confidentiality obligation clauses in bids or proposals; such documents often contain pricing formulas or other confidential information. If the customer disregards its obligation and releases the data, you may use the customer contract to get an injunction against use or further disclosure by the party who received the information from your customer.

Potential Acquirors

The potential acquiree must be even more cautious than the licensee. The potential acquiror will probably need to see all of your proprietary information to properly evaluate your business. Therefore, continue such discussions beyond the preliminary stage only with a strictly worded nondisclosure agreement. That agreement should stipulate the return of all materials in the event the purchase is not finalized. In addition, learn who will examine your trade secrets. Carefully monitor this process to determine whether the potential acquiror's personnel wish to evaluate your information, or to learn how to duplicate it. Record who examines what, and what is copied or extracted. As in dealing with prospective licensees, record complete and accurate minutes of all meetings especially where technical information is exchanged.

Potential acquirors must also maintain good records to prove the exact nature of the information received. Be keenly aware of your existing and planned technology, and of the industry technology, to better evaluate the potential acquiree's offer. Finally, avoid signing any nondisclosure agreement which may impede your development or exploitation of legitimately acquired technology.

Licensees

A dilemma lies in disclosing enough data to inform the potential licensee what you are selling, but not so much as to destroy its utility by failing to maintain the essential information as a secret. Like the prospective acquiror of your business, the prospective licensee may, in fact, only want to closely examine your operations and proprietary data. Disclose only *non-confidential* information prepared meticulously in advance. To ensure you make no mistakes, limit access to secure areas or information and secure maximum advantage from discussing publicly available information before proceeding to the next step.

Before disclosing any truly sensitive data to a potential licensee, always get a written nondisclosure agreement (see Appendix E). In addition, record full and accurate minutes of all meetings, until the license agreement is actually signed. If negotiations break down, act promptly and firmly to ensure return of all documentation and to remind the other party of its nondisclosure obligations.

No-Frills Protection

Few companies need or can afford to institute *all* of the procedures outlined in this chapter. What is right for you depends upon a balance of several factors.

- Importance of secrecy of the data.
- Employee turnover.
- Ability to review and enforce any particular procedures on a continuing basis.
- Cost weighed against the efficacy of any given method of protection.

If you are just starting out with a few employees, and have neither the time nor money to perform all the suggested procedures, here is a list of the *minimum* safeguards you should institute *from the beginning*:

- *Employment agreements* which provide for protection of proprietary data and disclosure of ideas.
- *"Confidential" stamps* for business plans, customer lists, drawings, and other technical data.
- *Nondisclosure agreements*, for vendors, customers, potential licensees, and the like.

SECRET

4
Unfair Competition

The vast majority of the lawsuits prosecuted in this country for "unfair competition" relate to customer list theft and employee raiding. Temporarily set aside the emphasis on technological issues and instead concentrate on issues pertinent to every American business, examining what constitutes acceptable competitive practices.

Many lawyers believe that customer list theft and employee raiding stimulate so much litigation because they are emotional issues. When a trusted employee or supplier improperly uses confidential technology, it is relatively easy to confront the suspect. The person is simply a thief, and should be dealt with accordingly. Lines are not so clearly drawn in soliciting customers and employees. The outrage reflects the frustration of knowing you've been had, while being unable to legally substantiate your claims to others.

In the area of technology and proprietary innovations, the lawsuit is largely left to the experts. After all, most judges have little training for independently resolving such issues. But, when a basic propriety of a competitive business practice is in question, the courts, as regular arbiters of what is equitable and just, enthusiastically join the debate without help from anyone else.

As a result, court decisions in these two areas are often inconsistent and are characterized by a heavy reliance on the "peculiar facts" of each case. In other words, the court will weigh the merits of your case on the appearance of unfair conduct by the opponent rather than on the application of legal "precedents." Advance planning and the proper approach to litigation can play a fundamental role in those cases that involve customer list theft and employee raiding.

Because the law here is uncertain, is still evolving, and often varies among courts and the states, you should not rely on specific rules. However, the courts have contributed several useful themes and general concepts. We will examine these, and consider some specific suggestions for planning against and reacting to these situations. First consider an example of how the courts have treated these issues in the past.

In the early 1960s many "national" insurance companies operated under the American Agency System. Licensed agents represented a number of different companies, offering competing lines to their customers. One company, the American Republic Insurance Company, shifted to an exclusive agency system. It created regional and local organizations of agents who sold exclusively American policies. The agents were given significant sales incentives and were provided with leads for prospective customers resulting from regional and national advertising campaigns conducted by the company.

In late 1966, Union Fidelity Life Insurance Company set up a system similiar to American's, offering exclusive area franchises to experienced agents willing to sell Union's product exclusively. To implement the most efficient system possible, Union planned to recruit area managers from other insurance companies and communicated with one of American's regional managers, LeRoy Lindgren.

In February 1967, Lindgren responded to the inquiry by completing a questionnaire, noting that 27 agents worked under his direction. Later that month, a telephone conversation between Lindgren and Alfred Coletta, an officer of Union, took place. Coletta expressed Union's intent to attract managers "who have an agent's following." Lindgren replied that he felt he could retain "a good 90% of the organization." By mid-April, Lindgren had signed an employment contract with Union but did not resign from American until two weeks later. During that interval he tried to pursuade those working for him to leave and join Union. Finally, when he submitted his own resignation, he terminated every agent who worked for him in American's organization.

Lindgren brought 15 of the former American agents to Union, but that was not all. He also retained "customer lead cards" and other information American had provided him for soliciting business.

A federal court found that both Lindgren and Union had conspired to commit unfair competitive practices. Lindgren, as an American manager, had a duty to work only in American's interests while he was in its employ. His wholesale solicitation of American's employees was considered tantamount to stealing one of American's most important assets. And although the court noted, "there is no proprietary right to customers or proposed customers," it added that "a variety of theories" (but primarily breach of trust) can be used to justify prohibiting an employee from using a customer list developed by the employer at great expense. (*American Republic Ins. Co.* v. *Union Fidelity Life Ins. Co.*, Ninth Circuit U.S. Court of Appeals 1972, 470 F2d 820.)

American v. *Union* is especially significant for three reasons. First, the *timing* of Lindgren's actions in soliciting American's employees. Had he waited until after resigning from American, he might have done exactly what he did without punishment.

Second, not only the departing manager but also his *new employer* were found liable. Weigh the significance of this factor before you consider hiring away from a competitor. Unless you plan and control your solicitation of another's employees (as well as the material they bring), your plans may be halted. Expensive litigation could ensue, possibly resulting in damages being awarded (here, punitive damages were assessed against Union in addition to American's loss of profits).

Finally, the case demonstrated the importance of *proper documentation* in defending against a charge of improper solicitation. An unnecessary "paper trail" of evidence provided to American's lawyers showed that the solicitation was planned in advance and with Union's knowledge. Had it anticipated the litigation, this sort of damning evidence would not have existed. Indeed some useful, self-serving documents could have been created in the first place.

Customer Lists

Even more so than employee raiding, customer list disputes are characterized by high emotionalism. One author writes, "The difference between stealing an employer's [technology] trade secrets and taking his customers . . . is like the difference between stealing an employer's car and taking his wife, too."[1]

This emotionalism is the fuel that feeds the litigation in this area. It is derived from common misconceptions about applicable law. Many

[1]Liberstein, Stanley. *Who Owns What Is In Your Head? Trade Secrets & the Mobile Employee.* New York: Dutton, 1979.

employees believe it is perfectly proper to "take what's in my head" (a customer "list" need not be written to be protected). However, many employers believe departing employees have no right to use *anything* they have learned on the job.

But, the results in any particular case will depend on the specific facts. Precedents, although useful, will normally not be controlling. However, one thread ties together all customer list cases. Information concerning a business' customers is an *asset* of the business called *goodwill*. One court decision resulted in the clarification of that concept.

> "The fundamental difference in the decisions, as we read them, is whether in a given case the knowledge gained by an employee is secret and confidential. If it is, its use by a former employee will be enjoined. If it is not, its use by a former employee will not be enjoined. Some knowledge gained by an employee is of such a general character that equity will not restrict its later use. An employee has a right, after cessation of employment, to use anything that is not the property of his employer. Trade and business secrets and confidential information are the property of the employer and cannot be used by the employee for his own benefit. A list of subscribers of a service, built by ingenuity, time, labor, and expense of the owner over a period of many years is the property of the employer, a part of the goodwill of his business and, in some instances, his entire business. Knowledge of such a list, acquired by an employee by reason of his employment, may not be used by the employee as his own property or to his employer's prejudice." (*California Intelligence Bureau* v. *Cunningham*, California District Court of Appeal 1948, 83 CA2d 197)

Confidentiality vs. Availability

The courts will apply the basic theory that apart from the generally applicable skills any employee acquires in the course of employment, it is "unfair" for an ex-employee to use any *confidential* information learned during employment. Regarding technology, the courts generally give protection equivalent to the protection the employer has demonstrated *in practice*. A later section describes some specific steps to take to properly convey the value of your customer data.

What exactly will the courts protect? In certain cases, the actual identity of the customers is considered a protectable trade secret. In many others, the protected matter will be information about the customers, either separate or in conjunction with a "list" of their identities. Many court decision reports and legal writers do not focus on the distinction between these situations. However, it is a useful way to analyze the law and avoid some misconceptions which may arise from confusing the two.

The identity of customers is primarily at issue in the classical "customer list" or "route" case (the latter refers to a string of court decisions dealing with customers located along the route of a milk delivery truck). To treat this information as a trade secret, you might imagine the information must be secret. In fact, many courts do require it. But if you have taken reasonable steps within your operation to protect the confidentiality of your list (whether it is written or not), the actual standard becomes: Would the customer names be difficult to gather? Within any city, most individuals and virtually every business are listed in a telephone directory; the "secret" lies in the knowledge that a certain subset will purchase or continue to purchase the goods or services your business offers.

The quotation describing the general approach on customer lists came from a 1948 opinion in the case of *California Intelligence Bureau* v. *Cunningham*. A business gathered information over a long period of time, to determine real vs. fraudulent charities and sold this information by subscription to philanthropic, commercial, or civic organizations which were likely targets for charitable solicitations. Cunningham was employed to acquire new subscriptions for the service. In performing his duties over the years, he managed to secure 84 new customers. The relationship became strained and he quit, threatening as he left to destroy his former employer's business.

True to his promise, Cunningham set up a competing business and almost immediately secured for himself 80 of the accounts he had established for his ex-employer. The court issued an injunction against soliciting these subscribers since they constituted a "preferred list" of persons who, over the years, had been screened and identified as those most likely to purchase the service.

Thus, even if the names of the customers can be found among public lists, if the employer's list constitutes a subset of that information, that is, customers "preferred" for some reason, then that list is entitled to protection. As one moves from the retail to the wholesale marketplace, however, such a standard becomes difficult to meet. Wholesale customers are normally far fewer in numbers (potential and actual), and are easily identified from trade journals, directories, and the like. Moreover, because they often purchase similar goods from multiple suppliers, the ex-employer's business is less likely to be abandoned as a result of the ex-employee's solicitation, and the courts intervene less often.

It is important to distinguish between the "customer" and the "decision maker." While a corporate customer may be easily identified from public information, it may be difficult to determine which individual within the organization determines who gets the company's patronage (or how much of it) in a particular area. The identity of these individuals may constitute a protectable trade secret.

Remember, trade secrets are not necessarily exclusive. In the area of technology, several competitors may simultaneously hold the same trade secret which each independently discovered or otherwise acquired. The same is true of customer lists. An ex-employee has every right—assuming the absence of a valid noncompetition agreement—to solicit the former employer's customers if their identities are independently discovered (for example, an ex-employee could build the customer list "from scratch"—see Chapter 5 on this point—or the new employer could provide the names from its own list). Again it is appearances that count. If surrounding circumstances such as the speed or selectivity of the former employee's solicitation indicate to a court that a confidential customer list has been used, then the ex-employee may be enjoined, even though the list could have been created independently.

This was the situation in the New York case of *Arnold's Ice Cream Co.* v. *Carlson*, decided in 1971 (United States District Court for the Eastern District of New York, 330 F Supp 1185). Borden's had quit doing business in a portion of the New York market in 1969. Carlson and Messlow had been employed as truck drivers for Borden's, delivering to retail outlets. Arnold's hired them as part of a successful effort to capture a portion of Borden's abandoned business. After less than two years with Arnold's, Carlson and Messlow resigned without notice and began to compete through two corporations previously set up by their wives. For a period before their resignation, they solicited accounts from Arnold's customers, and in the last couple of weeks their sales volume fell off precipitously. As soon as they resigned, Arnold's immediately lost a large portion of the business that the defendants had serviced. Carlson and Messlow argued that the identity of the customers was not secret, to which the court responded,

> "It may well be that defendants could have compiled a list of customers similar to plaintiff's based on individual knowledge and access to pages in a telephone directory, but this does not appear to be the case here. The testimony before the court and the affidavits submitted by counsel indicate that defendants quickly and effectively solicited plaintiff's former customers and that defendants did not compile a list of their own, but relied upon plaintiff's previous efforts."

Would the results have been the same had Carlson and Messlow waited until after resigning to solicit Arnold's customers and had given appropriate notice before quitting? Perhaps. One would think that a trade secret should be protected from use under all circumstances. However, in practice the courts are profoundly affected by these "collateral" facts reflecting the gut-level "fairness" of the employee's actions. While it may not be necessary, it is extraordinarily useful to impress the judge or jury with how badly the defendants behaved in leaving and competing. And a successful defense against such a charge will largely depend on whether the ex-employees appear to have acted reasonably and without the intent to injure their former employer.

Assume that your customers' identities cannot possibly be protected as a trade secret, either because the information is readily available from other sources or because you have failed to take reasonable steps to protect it from improper disclosure. In this case, the courts will provide relief against the former employee, if you show that in addition to a customer's identity other confidential information concerning the customer is involved. Even though the identity of every purchaser of Widgets in the world is well known, your business may have developed information delineating which purchasers will buy and for what reasons. All salespeople and most judges know the difference between a cold call and a hot prospect. When an employee leaves knowing which potential customers constitute hot prospects, you may properly seek relief to stop the employee from using *that* information.

Objective Customer Information

Examples of objective customer information most often cited by the courts include a particular customer's needs, preferences, and buying habits. "Needs" refers to the customer's requirements for a particular quantity of product or service, or for a particular type of product or service within the line that you sell. As any salesperson will confide, it is easier to sell when you know the customer's exact needs.

"Preferences" include a customer's preferred mode of delivery (packaging, scheduling, or method of delivery such as leaving the paper on the porch instead of on the driveway). A customer's preference also includes collateral services regularly provided to the customer (for instance, invoices providing information specific to the customer's accounting system), the frequency of follow-up sales contacts expected by the customer, and special contract terms the customer normally accepts.

"Buying habits," perhaps the most significant of this information, include the expected volume of business, frequency of sales, and price sensitivity. All express *profitability*. When you know a competitor's most profitable customers, you can effectively compete, by concentrating your efforts solely on those accounts. When this information is used by one who acquired it in confidence, the courts can be expected to intervene.

Subjective Customer Information

The other general category of protectable customer information is described as "subjective" simply because the courts find it difficult to define. It relates generally to a customer's loyalties and friendship as factors in deciding whether to award or continue patronage. These issues are always more important in service (for example, financial planning, gardening) or service-oriented (for example, insurance) industries. An employee may have an acute perception of a customer's loyalty or lack of it. For example, a salesperson usually knows whether a customer is new, or has had a recent bad experience and is therefore "ripe" for a competitive solicitation or whether the customer has been well served by the business for a long time, is quite happy, and therefore not a good prospect.

As an employer seeking an injunction against use of this "subjective" information, you must demonstrate your exclusive relationship with the customer which would continue unless interfered with by the former employee. Personal friendship between the customer and the former employee is usually more significant than the customer's general loyalty to the business. When the employee changes jobs, the expectation of continued patronage (*your* asset) which depends upon that friendship is severely jeopardized.

You may technically build your case for an injunction by showing that your customers generally decide to do business with you because of such personal relationships, rather than price or quality considerations. In practice, however, it may be more difficult than you expected to obtain relief. In the the first place, judges seek to balance your property interest with the employee's right to pursue a chosen occupation. Judges do not like to take away someone's livelihood. Especially in the absence of evidence indicating evil motives harbored by the ex-employee, the court may regard prohibiting an individual from utilizing industry "contacts" as jeopardizing success in the chosen field. Secondly, your customer undoubtedly will very much appreciate the new competition regardless of whether it is "fairly conducted" from your point of view. This customer may become an effective witness against your case by recalling that the customer solicited the ex-employee and not vice-versa.

In Chapter 5, your employees and would-be competitors are instructed to carefully create their *own* customer list from publicly available sources, going step-by-step through the customer's organization until they "discover" the decision maker they've already known for years. This may seem a charade and is open to attack. If the "friendship factor" is the protectable asset, does it matter if the ex-employee diligently labored over this fictitious task? While that argument seems logically sound, most judges will reject it. The individual's actions have avoided the *appearance* of impropriety and to rule otherwise would simply freeze the person out of the chosen profession. This circumstance perfectly exemplifies how the law of unfair competition rests not on tightly constructed, consistent legal theories, but on the court's visceral judgment based on the apparent facts.

As difficult as these subjective factors become for the courts, they also present a significant challenge to the former employee who wishes to compete. Remember the ex-employee will formulate a defense to show that a customer's patronage is minimally influenced by personal relationships and is instead based on objective criteria such as price or quality of goods or services. In pursuing that defense, evidence will be gathered to demonstrate that your customers are basically fickle and that changing accounts, short relationships, and order cancellations are frequent. And in the volatile environment of the modern commercial world, that defense will usually succeed.

One court, in a leading decision, described it this way:

> "We are not confronted here with a situation . . . in which it appeared that the business of selling and serving the various customers of the employer was primarily a matter of friendly feeling between the customer and the employer on the route delivering the commodities sold or serviced. In the case of a salesman in a commercial field, there is no assurance of an order unless he can satisfy the customer that his merchandise is better, cheaper or more salable than that of his competitor. The customer usually desires to examine, inspect and compare merchandise and prices offered to him. Each sale is a distinct transaction, not necessarily implying that another will follow."
>
> (*Continental Car-Na-Var Corp.* v. *Mosely,* 1949, 24 Cal2d 104).

Another court, denying an injunction in a case dealing with a "highly competitive" industry, had this to say:

> "Equitable protection may be invoked against the subsequent use by an employee of knowledge of the 'peculiar likes and fancies and other characteristics' of the former employer's customers where such knowledge will aid him in

> securing and retaining their business. This rule applies where friendly contact with customers is important to solicitors, a circumstance of the so-called 'trade route' cases. It has also been applied to situations involving a knowledge of the customer's desire for specialized information, his preference for certain products, and his buying habits. However, where, as here, superiority of product or service, rather than personal relationships or a secret speciality is the basis for patronage, a knowledge of the customer's requirements is not sufficient reason for an injunction. Under circumstances of open competition, such knowledge is readily available to all in the trade."

The court's findings in this area so far seen inconsistent. Either the judges are not always aware of the real reasons behind their decisions, or they are not entirely honest in articulating them. Again, it is difficult to formulate strict standards for what constitutes unfair competition when the results so obviously follow the particular facts of each case. Some courts may require proof of the "friendly relationship" before they will protect certain customer information while others will not. The difference lies in the surrounding circumstances and how they are presented to the court. Those circumstances will include both the manner in which the former employee has separated and gone into competition, and the demonstrated value and confidentiality of the information.

Preventing Customer Raids

What can you do now to prevent or minimize the effect of a "raid" on your customers by a former employee? Develop evidence to guide a judge to conclude that your customer information should be protected. First, be sure that your customer lists include additional information about the needs, preferences, and buying habits of each particular customer. (A "list" is simply a customer record whether stored on paper, in computer files, or in someone's head.)

Require salespeople to keep records and submit reports concerning why they successfully sell to particular customers. While employed, the salespeople may confirm in writing that you can expect long, exclusive relationships with their customers. And they will most likely boast about the "special knowledge" used to close a sale. All of this information can haunt them at a later time, and contradict the predictable position they will take in court that they have not had access to proprietary business information. In addition, these reports and records should include the salesperson's careful projections of future expected sales to given customers. This sort of admission could assist enormously in litigation when one of your biggest headaches will be proving damages through lost sales.

Second, take reasonable steps to protect your lists and related confidential customer information. Supplement the following checklist with a thorough review of the material in Chapter 3 on trade secret protection in general.

- Divide knowledge of the information among enough employees to reduce the impact of the departure of any single employee.
- Regularly and extensively use confidentiality legends and stamps.
- Clearly and regularly educate your employees to know what you consider as confidential customer information and what their obligation is to protect it.
- Secure written contracts from sales, marketing personnel, and consultants acknowledging the existence of confidential customer information and promising to protect it from improper use or disclosure. Of course, where permitted, consider the possibility of a noncompetition agreement; however, don't demand more protection—in terms of time or geographical area—than you actually need. The courts frown on overreaching in these contracts, and even a limited restriction will profoundly affect an employee's ability to seek competitive employment or begin a competitive business.

Third, keep accounting records which permit retrieving periodic marketing, advertising, and other goodwill-generating campaign expenses on short notice. Keep in mind that the courts, in deciding whether to allow protection at all, carefully measure the value of the information by the *cost* of producing it. In many businesses, these numbers can be staggering and can disproportionately affect a judge who must rapidly decide whether to issue a temporary injunction.

Finally, always act quickly when an employee with access to confidential customer information leaves. Aggressive action in protecting your business assets will be a practical lesson for remaining employees, and discourage them from making plans for trading in proprietary data. Moreover, litigation and threats of litigation can have a collateral effect on your customers, encouraging them to stay in the fold in spite of the new solicitations. However, consider this risk as well: Some customers may avoid involvement by giving business to neither side. Indeed some may perceive your actions as efforts to stifle legitimate competition and may be more receptive to your former employee's solicitation.

Before concluding the discussion of customer lists, three issues should be considered: suppliers, special legislation, and solicitation.

Suppliers. The courts do not yet generally accept claims for improper use of confidential information concerning suppliers rather than customers. Such claims have been made in the trial courts, and at least provide additional evidence of inappropriate competitive conduct. Businesses often spend significant time and money to develop a coterie of vendors. These may be selected for their facilities, products and service characteristics, which are as difficult to determine as is a customer's "needs, preferences, and buying habits." In addition, suppliers are often involved in technology trade secret claims, since they are regularly given access to secret formulas, drawings, designs, tooling, and the like. An ex-employee's choice of identical suppliers for a competitive business may or may not be unfair by itself, but will often provide evidence of an attempt to use the former employer's proprietary technology.

Special Legislation. Review the statutes enacted in your state for any special legislation enacted to protect confidential customer information in your industry. Such a statute was recently enacted in California, giving special protection to personnel recruiters. It declares that the identity of all customers serviced within a six-month period prior to an employee's termination constitutes a "trade secret."

Solicitation. In customer list cases, the courts normally regard solicitation as the improper act by the former employee and will not interfere with the acceptance of unsolicited business. What constitutes solicitation therefore, is often an issue. Clearly, when the customer learns of the new competition and solicits your former employee's business, there can be no claim of unfair competition. What happens when the ex-employee merely announces a new affiliation to your customers without specifically asking for their patronage? The answer is not so straightforward. Some courts have taken the view, especially in earlier cases, that merely sending announcements did not constitute "solicitation." This was held to be the rule though the announcements were sent to customers from a confidential list. Other courts have taken a different view, holding that sending announcements necessarily implies a request for patronage and it is unfair to allow an employee to make *any* use of a confidential customer list. If you are concerned with the propriety of that type of activity by your employees or if you are considering competing with your present employer, consult with counsel to determine the rule in your own jurisdiction.

Employee Raiding

Your employees' loyalties are divided among their families, churches, ethnic groups, organizations, you, and others. And within your organization, loyalties are further divided. Although most have a general sense of loyalty to the company or their particular unit, many employees feel a primary allegiance to another individual within the organization. Perhaps they knew each other at an earlier job, and one helped the other get this one. Perhaps the individual simply has a certain quality of leadership. And more ominously, the individual may be the one among them who can articulate (and perhaps encourage) whatever feelings of dissatisfaction or frustration they have at work. It is the latter situation which most frequently produces employee raiding, or "predatory hiring."

The actual hiring may be done by an established competitor of yours or it may be the work of the "leader" who has left and established an independent organization. In either case, one or two central figures usually encourage a large group of employees to quit their jobs and join a competing group within a brief period of time.

Perhaps the most famous decision in this area is *Bancroft-Whitney Company* v. *Glen*, a California case decided in 1966. The opinion was the culmination of a five-year battle between Bancroft-Whitney, a West Coast publisher of law books, and its primary East Coast competitor, Matthew Bender & Co. At issue was Bender's wholesale recruiting of a large portion of Bancroft-Whitney's editorial staff.

Bancroft-Whitney's president, Judson B. Glen, had been with the company more than 20 years. However, in 1960, a management change at the parent company of Bancroft-Whitney led to a significant loss of the control that Glen had exercised over the business and he became dissatisfied. Rumors of that dissatisfaction reached a Bender manager, who made a confidential contact with Glen. They met in San Francisco, and discussed the possibility of Glen's establishing a western division for Bender. Glen was receptive. Since a sales manager would be needed for the new organization, and Glen suggested that Bender contact Baker, Bancroft-Whitney's regional sales manager for Los Angeles (and a member of its board of directors). That contact was made and Baker also indicated some interest. Thereafter, in spite of rumors to the contrary, Glen assured his superiors that he and Baker had no interest in leaving to join Bender.

Glen eventually resigned his position on December 15, 1961, having previously signed a contract to begin working for Bender at the beginning of the next year. In the preceding month, however, he had actively solicited many of his own company's editors and managing editors to leave with him. In addition, he gave Bender specific information about the salaries and other benefits those employees received, enabling Bender to approach them directly with slightly increased salary offers. Finally, during this period he actively advised Bender which Bancroft-Whitney employees would be most useful and most likely to accept offers if solicited to leave.

In finding liability against Glen, the court noted that there is no general requirement that an officer or manager divulge to an employer any plans to leave and enter competitive employment, provided, however, that the employee's secrecy does not cause some particular harm to the company. Here, Glen had lulled his superiors into a false sense of security concerning their ability to retain a major portion of their staff. Moreover, he had recommended a delayed salary increase to the Bancroft-Whitney management, which made it easier to recruit their employees. Finally, he had used the special knowledge he had about the Bancroft-Whitney editors for a purpose which ran counter to the company interests. In essence, he failed to disclose he was working primarily for a competitor during the last several months of his employment. Certainly, the court said, Glen's failure to disclose these facts was extremely harmful to the company. The decision said,

> "It is beyond question that a corporate officer breaches his fiduciary duties when, with the purpose of facilitating the recruiting of the corporation's employees by a competitor, he supplies the competitor with a selective list of the corporation's employees who are, in his judgment, possessed of both ability and the personal characteristics desirable in an employee, together with the salary the corporation is paying the employee and a suggestion as to the salary the competitor should offer in order to be successful in recruitment. This conclusion is inescapable even if the information regarding salaries is not deemed to be confidential."

In the *Motorola* v. *Fairchild* case (reviewed in Chapter 3), the court found no liability for the "raiding" of Motorola's semiconductor division employees. Yet one of the defendants and departing employees, who was a senior officer and director of Motorola, had given Fairchild the names of several employees they might solicit, together with suggested salary ranges and stock options, while still working for Motorola.

The judge explained the result this way. Each of the employees had good reasons independent of Fairchild's solicitation to leave his or her job. No evidence of any conspiracy among the defendants to injure Motorola existed, and each of the individuals contacted Fairchild directly and independently. Finally, each was readily replaced with a competent substitute. Motorola was therefore unable to prove that it had been damaged as a result of the defendant's actions, no matter how improper they might have appeared.

With these and other seemingly inconsistent decisions, some conclusions still can be drawn that will apply to most predatory hiring situations. Generally, the courts consider certain hiring practices to be unfair competition. In applying these basic rules, the courts will "balance" the equities of each situation and focus their attention on the surrounding facts and circumstances as they appear to them.

The courts consider the following to be unfair hiring practices:

- Hiring of a company's employees by a former officer or manager who has had access to and used particular information concerning the employees' names, abilities, and compensation packages.
- Hiring away a group of employees as a means to impair substantially or destroy a competitor's ability to compete in a given market. (This conduct may also violate federal and state antitrust laws.)
- Hiring employees to acquire a competitor's confidential technology or business information.

The courts will consider the rights of all parties involved, including

- The employee's right to seek new employment and to use the general knowledge and skills gained in the old;
- The new employer's right to avail itself of the employee's skills; and
- The ex-employer's demonstrated interest in the protection of its confidential information, in the loyalty of its present employees and especially in its ability to survive as a viable competitor in the face of mass staff defections.

These competing interests are rarely academically examined by a judge. Instead, they are weighed in the context of how disloyal and generally evil the first two parties have been, how badly the third has been damaged as a result, and the adequacy of the proof of those charges.

How can you tell if raiding is realistically a potential problem for you? If your industry is characterized by intense competition within a relatively small geographic area, your competitors are likely to consider you a source for incremental staffing. This is especially true in industries characterized by easy entry and high growth rates. If you find yourself without substantial competition, your area may be targeted for a new entrant. And, like the East Coast competitor of Bancroft-Whitney, that competitor will probably consider creating its ranks of personnel from yours. These factors are exacerbated by the acceptance of employee mobility and security in "job hopping." And finally, consider yourself a sitting duck if you are experiencing severe morale problems because of inadequate benefits or any other reason.

You may discover a raid too late to take any effective countermeasures. Therefore, keep as close to the rumor mill as possible in order to maximize your warning time. Certainly be alert to the departure of an officer or key manager, especially when the separation is less than amicable and when the employee will not discuss future plans. Once the "leader" leaves, you may either experience a precipitous departure of several "followers" or a trickle of voluntary terminations. Employees may go to work for a single competitor, or refuse to indicate their plans as they leave. Even if no terminations immediately follow the manager's departure, you may sense a continuing uneasiness among the employees who were loyal to the manager, somewhat like the quiet before a storm.

When things have progressed to that point, your options are severely limited. Even if you can identify the likely targets of solicitation, their minds may have been so poisoned that your entreaties will be largely ignored. If a "conspiracy" is afoot, you will be perceived as the "enemy."

Preventing Employee Raiding

What long-range plans can help prevent employee raiding? First, continuously consider your wages, fringe benefits, and the non-monetary rewards used to motivate your staff. After all, satisfied employees have no reason to defect. Next, identify your confidential managers and officers, and the employee information they have access to. If possible, secure a written agreement (perhaps as a part of the employment or confidential information agreement) from each of those persons not to solicit employees of the company on behalf of a competitor, or to divulge any employee information to a competitor. At least warn each of them in writing of their obligation to always and solely act in the company's interest, and of their obligation, even after termination of their employment, to protect as confidential all employee information and not to use it in any way which might harm the company.

Restrict access to information regarding the names, salary, and benefits of your employees. Store and lock all of this information within a professional central personnel department and make it available to managers only as periodically needed for employee reviews. In particular, be aware of recruiters' attempts to collect this information. Especially dangerous, they act on behalf of anonymous clients and make it harder to discover a raid at an early stage, than when the competitor acts directly.

Remember to keep your security tight for visitors, vendors, customers, and others who might have access to company facilities or functions where this information could be collected. Identify competitors who may have a particular need for a group within your staff. Your personnel department can help you by monitoring the help wanted advertisements placed by the competition in newspapers or trade journals.

Keep close tabs on the informal "information flow" at your facilities, to discover potential problems which could lead to a raid. Prepare to act when a particularly significant officer, manager, or a member of an important "team" joins a new or established competitor. Watch for signs that others may be considering following. Create and implement a contingency plan to fight aggressively against a raid the moment it becomes evident.

If you do perceive that a raid might occur or may already be in progress, you must act quickly. If targeted employees remain, you may be able to convince them to stay with the company. And if the already-departed employees are considering soliciting others, your actions at this juncture may change *their* minds and convince them to stop. Also, should you consider threatening or bringing litigation against someone, it is at this point when the damage appears most obvious. If you wait until you have replaced most of the raided employees, the court may find that your damage is not continuing, though your new employees work less effectively. If your damage is not continuing, you may not win an injunction, a far more effective remedy than money damages. (See Chapter 6 on litigation.)

Immediately identify those who left together and those who may be solicited. As to the latter, develop a plan to save those worth saving and consider dismissing those who are not, or who might cause greater damage should they stay. Place the departed employees and their new employer on notice of your intention to pursue legal action if the raid does not immediately stop (see Appendices B and C for examples of typical warning letters). Act under the advice of counsel, but by all means, act aggressively and with speed. A letter or phone call from a lawyer will show you mean business. Once the raid gains momentum, it will be difficult to stop.

Documenting the Raid

During all of this activity, you must compile complete and accurate documentation of events as they occur. On a daily basis, record conversations, perceptions, and impressions that could assist in planning your defensive strategies. Such records will be invaluable should you pursue a lawsuit. Be especially careful to adequately document exit interviews during this period. Obtain as much information as possible concerning the employee's reasons for leaving and future plans. This information will probably be false, and although it is no crime to lie to an ex-employer, a lie will significantly impact a judge or jury.

After identifying those who are likely to leave, consider putting them under in-house surveillance. Document any unusual and frequent telephone calls, conferences, and excessive time away from the facilities. In addition, observe excessive use of copying facilities and frequent removal of "work to take home." Remember, until a raid concludes, you may be essentially operating with the competition's spies in your midst. If fortunate enough to discover hard evidence of that fact, you can immediately terminate those involved and confront the new competitor with the situation, which should abruptly halt further recruiting activities.

Begin early to document the impact of the defections. Winning an injunction will largely depend on your ability to demonstrate specific harm to your company or project group. And you'll need this later when it will be harder to reconstruct to prove damages. Keep a separate file with continuing calculations and descriptions of the raid's effects, such as project disruptions, delays, and your out-of-the-pocket costs incurred in trying to minimize those effects. Recoverable costs can include recruiting fees, training costs, premiums for temporary help, overtime wages, and the like.

Documentating Fair Recruiting

What if, on the other hand, you are considering hiring a group of employees from a competitor and want to minimize the chance of being sued? Again, consider the several theories upon which the courts base liability for raiding. You may hire away your competitor's employees so long as your methodology does not effectively destroy an ability to compete, or you do not use confidential information supplied by the competitor's employees, or you do not hire employees to secure the competitor's proprietary technology or confidential business information.

At the outset, write job descriptions and requisitions describing the positions you need to fill. Emphasize the objective attributes and general experience level of the personnel you hope to hire and avoid naming particular persons or indicating a desire to acquire specific information through them. Consider using a professional recruiter, on a negotiated basis, to solicit the desired employees. Third party activities will often throw the competitor off your scent and make it difficult to exactly determine the source of the hiring effort. However, the recruiter should not hire everyone from the same company or your ruse will be quite transparent.

When you have hired employees from a competitor, warn them, before they enter your premises, not to bring any papers generated while working for your competitor (do this as a part of the entrance interview described in Chapter 3). Require them to sign documents affirming that they have not brought such information with them, that you intend to rely on their assurance in that regard, and that you are employing them for their abilities, and not for their knowledge of anyone's confidential information or for their ability to solicit other employees.

You may want to create and document a special position for an employee who has held a particularly sensitive position with a competitor. During this "incubation period" the employee would not be exposed to similar projects at your facilities or otherwise put in a position which might compromise any of the former employer's confidential information. This is essential for a group of employees who worked together for the competitor. They will probably continue to discuss and share information among themselves about the previous employer's projects.

Consider writing the former employer a letter indicating that you have hired this employee and intend to take all necessary steps to protect any confidential information which the employee may have as a result of the prior employment. This type of contact will often imply goodwill and will forestall possible litigation. Moreover, it forces the former employer to respond quickly. If you integrate the employee inextricably into your organization before the former employer acts, the court may find the employer has waived any claim against you as a result of the hire.

HUMMEL

5
Competing With a Former Employer

If you are considering striking out on your own, you probably turned to this chapter directly from the Table of Contents. Don't stop here; read the whole book. Learning the perspective of your employer will help you plan and execute your move and deter a potential suit. More important, if things go well, you will soon be an employer yourself. The time to start protecting *your* trade secrets is now.

And, if you are in management, and can't imagine leaving the company, chances are some of your employees may already have considered leaving. Some have made the decision to go and are planning their move now. In most cases, you won't be able to change their minds, and in some cases, you may not want to. But if you don't know how to recognize the signs, you will miss any chance to keep and convince valuable employees that their best opportunities lie with the company. In addition, learning how employees leave will help you design countermeasures to minimize the damages they cause on the way out.

Planning the Move

People who want to leave and compete with their employer can be categorized by their primary motive for leaving. The "Bruised Ego," for example, is very angry, having been passed over for promotion, plagued by ignored or rejected ideas, or suffered from the innumerable political assassinations that occur in the corporate environment. The Bruised Ego wants to leave to show the company, boss, or fellow employees that he or she doesn't need them and, in fact, can run circles around them in the marketplace.

The second type is the "True Adventurer," who decides to move because of the potential opportunity outside. A True Adventurer may be pushed in that direction by insufficient salary, recognition, or opportunity within the company. But the primary motive is what the employee can get, rather than what she or he is leaving.

Actually, most people find themselves to be some combination of these two. Recognizing where your tendencies lie will alert you to potential problems with your attitude toward planning your move. If you are a Bruised Ego, you will probably ignore careful preparation in favor of a quick and dramatic exit. And if you are a True Adventurer, you may feel that planning your move while you're still working for the company is somehow unethical.

Deliberate, careful planning of your new enterprise is neither illegal nor immoral. In fact, unless you are independently wealthy, you must do it now, while you still have an income and before you burn any bridges. As long as you don't actually begin your competing business or start recruiting your team from your employer's staff while still on the payroll, you should be in the clear. The following section offers essential considerations in laying out your plan. Remember, however, that other factors peculiar to your situation may also be significant. Ask yourself frequently what can possibly go wrong? Plan for those contingencies.

Reviewing Company Obligations

If you're an officer, director, or manager, you may have special, more stringent obligations not to jeopardize the company or deprive it of a business opportunity. This "fiduciary duty" continues at least until you have resigned, and in some respects goes on indefinitely.

There are two things you must consider. First, take extreme care in hiring other employees of the company. Wait until after you have resigned. Make it clear that you are not recruiting in order to gain access to the company's trade secrets, to eliminate it as a competitor, or to harm it in any way. And when you do start to hire, *record* your efforts in detail. Maintain a file on each applicant, showing (as appropriate)

- The employee's application for the job (for example, through an unsolicited request to you).
- How you got the employee's name if you solicited.
- The information regarding compensation, benefits, and expertise; you must elicit this data in the interview, regardless of whether you already know it.

• The employee's agreement not to bring any confidential information belonging to the former employer (see Appendix F). This last provision is often overlooked or ignored, either because there is a silent assumption that the new employee wouldn't do anything wrong, or because the employee insists on keeping notes, work samples, or forms. However, a completely clean hire which is well-documented is extremely important in a lawsuit because it underscores your appearance as a fair competitor.

Second, carefully examine whether your new enterprise constitutes a "corporate opportunity" which you must first offer to the company before you can pursue it. Surprisingly, such offers are frequently rejected, providing excellent insurance against later litigation. However, if your idea presents extraordinary possibilities, you may not want to follow this course. In any event, this area of the law varies significantly among states, and is rapidly changing; you would do well to consult a lawyer on this point.

If you have special access to important technology or business information, the company's concerns are first, that you not use it in your new position, and second, that you leave it in a form that others can continue to use. If you have access to this type of information, for example as a research engineer, marketing executive, or controller, you are in a special position with duties similar to those of an officer or director. Return all company documents you may have and keep a log of them, if practical. Prepare papers, drawings, and notebooks for those who will take over your duties. If they know everything is obviously there and that you organized a smooth transition, they will have no reason to suspect you of any wrongdoing and you will have lessened the chance of being sued (in fact, you may be asked to consult part-time on uncompleted projects).

A possible problem is the employment or inventions agreement. This may include a clause requiring you to sign over to your employer the rights to all inventions you conceive within a given period after your employment. In many jurisdictions these agreements are enforceable. If you are subject to one, consult a qualified lawyer at the earliest possible time. Advance planning in this area could easily mean the difference between lucrative success and expensive failure.

If you have a noncompetition agreement, you may be prohibited from competing with the employer for some time after termination. Some states—notably California—prohibit such agreements except under strictly defined circumstances. (See Chapter 3 for a thorough discussion of these agreements.) This subject requires specialized legal advice. If you plan your new enterprise without considering a noncompetition contract, you may find the entire effort wasted, since most courts will quickly issue an injunction against a clear violation of the agreement.

If you plan ahead with qualified legal counsel you may develop strategies to avoid applying the agreement, as by designing your enterprise so it does not specifically compete with your employer. Or you may be able to attack the agreement directly by demonstrating that your employer has breached an obligation to you, excusing you from the noncompetition clause, or that the agreement was signed under duress or false pretenses. Several possibilities exist; explore them early in the planning stage to allow time to research and prepare an approach. This applies equally to other post-employment contract restrictions, such as a clause prohibiting association with employees, solicitation of customers, or a provision requiring assignment of inventions created after employment.

Initiating New Obligations

The Business Plan. When you plan a new enterprise, defining your project accurately and in great detail is critical. Take time to examine the market carefully. Talk to outsiders who know the industry, and especially to those who have experienced a start-up. Prepare a business plan even if you don't intend to raise money initially.[1] Circulate it among trusted friends for their candid comments; then write it, several times if necessary, until you feel you know exactly what your goals are and exactly what will make your business succeed. Concentrate on how to make your company different from—and better than—your present employer, who will initially be your stiffest competition.

Financial Preparation. If you are a Bruised Ego, be especially cautious in this area. Your inclination may be to cut the cord too quickly before you've had an opportunity to think it through. Examine the exact nature of the enterprise and its expected competition to determine your financial needs. Be conservative. Don't overestimate income or underestimate expenses. Be prepared to pay for borrowing if necessary, and see the bank to arrange for a credit line before you leave your employer. If your plans are more ambitious, check the availability of other financing

[1] For a helpful, straightforward discussion of how to write a good business plan (as well as how to overcome some of the common problems in starting a new business), see Donald M. Dible's, *Up Your Own Organization* (Entrepreneur Press, Fairfield, CA, 1974).

sources. If you scramble for equity investment after you've started, you will suffer a much greater dilution of your equity in the company than if you had made these contacts earlier. Many venture capitalists will help you plan your venture and define your business plan. However, carefully consider what to include in the plan; you and the venture capitalist could end up in litigation generated by your employer.

Check out your accrued vacation pay, bonuses, stock options, and the like. A short delay in leaving may offer some financial benefit, and, at this point, you'll need all the extra cash you can get. Don't depend on giving notice and working during that period. Frequently, employees who give notice are ushered immediately out the door, especially if they work with sensitive proprietary data. Depending on your employment contract or state law, you may not be entitled to any pay in lieu of notice.

Finally, develop a bail-out plan. Despite your best efforts in advance planning, too many things can go wrong. Establish various alternatives in case the unthinkable occurs. Remember, half of all businesses fail within the first five years, and most of these fail without the built-in disability of competing with an established former employer.

Protecting Your Plan

Do everything possible to keep your plan a secret from your employer until you are ready to give notice. Here the True Adventurer has the greatest problem, too excited about the new opportunity and less inclined than the Bruised Ego to be stealthy about it. Don't give in to temptation and be sure that any others who plan to leave with you also keep things under wraps. This avoids the unnecessary and embarrassing confrontation with superiors who might ask you to leave before you are ready. One possible exception involves an exercise of judgment as to the appropriate strategy. If a group of people plan to leave at the same time, it is useful to give the employer notice well in advance. The shocked and enraged employer will frequently react by firing the entire group on the spot and filing suit, irrespective of merit. Assuming you can withstand the financial impact of that circumstance, it will assist your defense of any raiding claim, since the employer can hardly complain of having created the difficult staffing situation.

When you break the news, continue to be circumspect about your specific plans. You have no obligation to say what you're going to do and if you're polite about it, your reluctance will usually not itself be enough to precipitate a lawsuit. Be as thoughtful, gracious, and cooperative as you can force yourself to be. Show your supervisor or manager the projects you have in progress, describe what needs to be done and offer whatever assistance you can to lessen the impact and burden of your leaving. As discussed earlier, a demonstrated desire to leave behind all company property and to facilitate an orderly transition is perhaps the best way to stay out of court.

As you leave or prepare to leave, you may be asked to sign a document acknowledging that you are not taking any confidential or proprietary information. This may happen even if you have previously signed a nondisclosure agreement. Indeed, your employer may urge you to sign it to confirm compliance with your contract. Normally, no legal reason requires you to sign such a document since your employment is now over (at worst, they'll ask you to leave earlier). In practice though, your "cooperation" may convince your employer that you present no threat, and decrease the chances of a suit.

In most cases, however, you are probably better off by politely declining the request. Most forms used by employers (for an example see Chapter 3 on exit interviews) require you to admit that confidential information exists and that you have had access to it. If a lawsuit does ensue, this paper could become a difficult piece of evidence (the issue most frequently disputed in trade secret litigation and often the most useful defense is whether the employer's information qualifies for trade secret protection).

While you refuse to sign, do reassure your employer that you intend to honor all your obligations. Your objective is to avoid being sued. Anything you can do to demonstrate your responsible view of the situation will help to accomplish that goal. You might address a letter to your manager containing the following information:

Dear ______:

As I was preparing to leave last Friday, you asked me to sign a "separation agreement" [use the title of the proposed document]. I declined and would like to explain why. The main reason is that my job is now over and it just doesn't seem right to be signing such a thing. Frankly, it reads just like it was written by a lawyer and that makes me uneasy. I want to tell you in my own words, though, that I intend to honor all my obligations to you and not to use any trade secrets that you may own. Please don't think that my hesitation about signing your particular form implies anything else.

The "separation agreement" referred to "trade secrets, proprietary, and confidential information." As I said, I certainly don't want to use anything that's yours, but I have a problem with how vague those words are. I would appreciate it if you could write me back and let me know just what *are* the "secrets" and "information" that you feel belong to you and which I've had access to. In that way, I can make my plans more intelligently and not have to guess at what your trade secrets might be.

I look forward to hearing from you.

Best regards,

Notice that the letter says "in my own words." Write in your own language, using this form only as a guide. You'll be more convincing, and if the letter ever becomes evidence, a jury will be more impressed by it. Also notice that in the second paragraph you want the employer to *define* its trade secrets. Even if the company has an excellent trade secrets program, clearly defining the information which you accessed in your job is a task that your former manager is not likely to do. So what happens? Your request is ignored—you'll almost never receive an adequate specification in response. And if you are ignored, a judge is unlikely to issue a trade secrets injunction against you. Since you have put the employer on notice of your need for a definition, the former employer cannot, in fairness, remain silent while you spend time and money to start your business or begin a new job.

Legally, the former employer is blocked from claiming violation of its trade secret rights. Use only the second paragraph of the letter if you have not been requested to sign a "separation agreement" but if the company has given a written or oral "reminder" of your confidentiality restrictions (see Appendix B for a sample "warning" letter).

Of course, your situation may be more directly antagonistic. If you believe a lawsuit is probable, don't hesitate to get qualified legal advice before terminating, if possible. What you and your employer write and say during this period can become important evidence and a lawyer can assist in phrasing and timing communications to maximize their value in court.

In fact, you must record everything that occurs during this period, in case a suit does follow. This applies to all your pretermination activities. Keep a log of dates, times, places, and names, and make permanent notes of all significant conversations. Remember that records are to litigation what location is to real estate. Whether you're in court and trying to prove what happened or whether you're in an adversary negotiation with your former employer before a suit is filed, the side with the superior documentation will usually prevail.

Starting Up While On the Payroll

It is not illegal to prepare to compete with your employer before leaving your present job. Strictly adhere to a few simple rules, and you can accomplish the objectives already discussed in this chapter *before* you change jobs or start your enterprise. Even if your employment contract appears to prohibit you from moonlighting or competing with your employer, you are entitled to take certain preparatory steps.

First, be sure everything you do is only in *preparation* for doing business, and not actually *doing* business. You can lease office space, reserve a phone number, print business cards, announcements and stationery, rent furniture, and the like. You normally must do things before opening your doors. But, you should *not* actually begin business, either by ordering material, pre-selling customers, creating product plans, or hiring employees.

Second, don't let your efforts interfere with your present employment. Remember, whatever the terms of your employment contract, you owe your employer a full day's work. You will not prove your indispensability to the world and you may provoke a lawsuit, if you make your peers or superiors look bad by leaving a significant amount of unfinished work. Finish all projects that you can, eliminating potential arguments that you planned to harm the company by leaving. Use accrued vacation days or evenings to accomplish your planning activities. Don't work on your business plans in your office on company time or using your company secretary. When it's time to give notice, do it in writing and offer to stay on or consult to provide a smooth transition. Your offer will probably be rejected anyway and it provides excellent evidence of your good intentions.

Third, don't use anything that belongs to your employer. Don't use logos or products from your employer or even anything similar to those used or sold by your employer. To do otherwise simply adds to the resentment of those you leave behind, and acts as a red flag to encourage a lawsuit. Don't keep anything at home or at your new office which you produced while working for your present employer even if you wish to keep it only as work samples. Leave material at your present office and prepare it to turn over to your superiors when you are ready to give notice.

Fourth, don't start building your new staff from the ranks of your present employer before you leave. Isolated hypothetical conversations are acceptable but anything more may be viewed as a large-scale recruiting "conspiracy." Once you have left, those who feel a loyalty to you will probably approach you for potential employment in your new venture and there is certainly nothing wrong with accepting their solicitation. In addition, you may require few people initially, and it is illogical to pay salaries for unproductive time. During this critical time, if approached by members of your present staff, simply thank them for their interest and explain that you cannot respond to their request until you have departed. Then note the solicitation in your records for later reference and follow-up.

If several people want to follow you, however, substantial pressure may be placed on them when the news breaks. Often your former employer will determine who is "targeted" and may immediately begin strenuous efforts to talk them into staying. Or worse, an injunction may be sought to stop you from hiring additional employees from the company. What do you do, hire them all right away? It is not only expensive, but increases the chance of litigation because the employer has clearly been hurt. Many courts will view such an act as strong evidence of your intent to harm the company by causing a precipitous loss of staff.

On the other hand, some courts have a considered "stretched-out" hiring program as evidence of evil motive. You want to maintain "spies" within the old organization to provide confidential information as it develops. You want to put your former employer at an unfair advantage by having it feed and clothe your "inventory" of future employees, and you will pick them off only as your business requires them. This ambivalent attitude of the judiciary offers no clear guidance. In general, however, consider these ordered factors in determining when to hire former fellow employees:

- Your business needs.
- The likeley responsive action of your former employer (including the potential of seeking and securing an injunction at any given point).
- The possible implications of your timing as evidence of intent to injure.

You will need to balance these considerations, along with the possibility of avoiding litigation completely, by recruiting employees from other sources.

Creating Your Own Technology

If you haven't already done so, read the preceding chapters carefully to learn what motivates employers to sue their employees. Avoid doing those things, or even creating the appearance of doing those things. Consider how to establish and protect your own trade secrets. Create a protection plan early, and stick to it religiously.

Objectively analyze and define your employer's technology, and the marketplace(s) in which you will be competing. Distinguish what you have learned about your job generally, from what you have learned by accessing your employer's special trade secrets. By answering these questions, you can more effectively direct your energies toward pursuing a technology with a minimized litigation risk. Focus on technology distinct from your employer's, which is applied in different markets, and/or which derives primarily from your skill and "know-how," rather than from the unique and secret designs and processes of your employer. Even if this cannot be totally accomplished, focusing on it will help create the appearance of a different technology. In this area of the law, as we have seen, appearances are critical.

Properly examine what the company might claim as its proprietary information. What constitutes its real technology or business data? What has it consistently tried to protect? Pursue this inquiry to understand what areas to avoid in your new venture and to glean information of potential value in a lawsuit. In court, the company must demonstrate it took reasonable measures to guard against disclosure of the claimed secrets. And although I don't suggest it as a deliberate high-visibility strategy, you may help the company to properly "publish" certain information before you leave. Certainly, you cannot improperly disclose confidential data to a third party and then claim that as a result of your illegal act, it is now available to you in the public domain. However, consider legitimate opportunities to encourage publication such as in promotional material or technical magazines, where the exposure arguably serves the company's interest.

Pursuing "me too" technology, even if you believe it does not violate your employer's proprietary rights, may dangerously invite litigation based on the mere suspicion of trade secrets theft. Therefore, try to differentiate your technology from that of your employer's, especially in the intended market. Clearly, your primary objectives are to develop your business and avoid litigation. A differentiated product creates greater recognition in the marketplace and presents less of a threat to your former employer, who will be less inclined to invest resources in a lawsuit.

Even if your technology undoubtedly differs in substance, don't stop there. Do everything possible to make it appear substantially different, especially to the layperson. A judge's eyes often glaze over during the thorough analysis and comparison of two mechanisms, but a judge can immediately see whether they *look* similar or seem to do similar things. This immediate impression is critical, and given the opportunity, design your product to affect that first impression.

You must keep accurate and complete records of the development of your technology. At any time, you must be able to re-create the process by which you conceived and developed your technology from scratch. The best proof of that effort consists of engineering notebooks, dated drawings, and other documents. Taken together they should provide a clear, written chronology of your independent work. Although expressed before, it bears repeating here: Do not, under any circumstances, either use or retain anything from your present employer and be sure adequate records show you returned all the material you have accessed.

Finally, protect your own technology, as described in Chapter 3. Don't be paranoid, but be extremely prudent in your business dealings with potential investors, customers, and vendors. Prepare nondisclosure agreements in advance of any discussion of your technology or marketing plans (see Appendices A and H). Conscientiously prepare a general description of your technology sufficient for the purpose of your meeting, without revealing the details of your own trade secrets. Disclose only enough information to venture capitalists and investors to create and maintain their interest, until they are sufficiently committed to justify a more complete disclosure. A conscientiously and professionally prepared business plan will describe your technology, and its intended exploitation, in carefully measured terms.

Creating Your Own Customer List

This is perhaps the easiest area in which to act preventatively and avoid litigation. Nevertheless, this subject area most frequently generates unfair competition litigation. Employers highly value the goodwill which they establish to ensure continued patronage from regular customers and they are enraged by the employee who "steals" that goodwill. Again, appearances are as important as the substance of your actions (generally see Chapter 4).

Identify and assess the marketplace and the types of customers it comprises. Determine the essential elements in their choice of suppliers of your goods or services. Customer trade which is based on personal service and friendship creates the greatest difficulty. Loyalties are difficult to change, and it is easily presumed that you could only obtain such a customer through improper means. On the other hand, customers who buy because of price, performance, or an objective measure of service are more easily obtained. With this type of customer, a court is less likely to assume that you have used information improperly, and more likely to conclude that your success reflects effective and fair competition and a superior product or service.

Focus your market analysis on how you identify potential customers. How many can be readily identified from "public" sources such as telephone books, trade publications, industry association mailing lists, and the like? The easier it is to make that identification the better. It is that much harder for your employer to claim the "list" as a trade secret. However, a distinction may be drawn—and usually is—between ready identification of a corporate customer and identification of the individual decision maker within the organization whose name may not be so easily discovered.

Two principles apply: *start* from scratch and *keep* complete records. Begin with a written analysis of the marketplace and potential customer groups, and with a list of possible public sources of names. As you review these sources and create your prospect list, prepare a separate "contact sheet" for each prospective customer (see Appendix I). On that sheet identify the customer by name, address, and telephone number, and indicate the public source of information. Fill in dates, names, and the content of conversations. The first recorded call on each contact sheet is the "cold" call where you telephone the customer's main office, gradually working your way from the receptionist to the decision maker, recording the names of everyone you speak with. Strictly follow this procedure, even if you know you will finally contact the same individual you have been talking and socializing with at trade shows for the past five years. It may seem absolutely silly and a waste of time but it will provide effective insurance against any charges that you have pirated customer information belonging to your former employer.

The entire effort is wasted, of course, if you keep your employer's customer lists. Therefore, leave all of that material at your present job. Remember, it is equally bad to take confidential information in your head as it is to take it on paper. Therefore, if you create any customer lists after you leave, be sure you can prove how you created them.

Of course, it is usually appropriate for the customer to solicit you. However, be sure to record that specific solicitation and to emphatically tell the customer that you cannot solicit business but that you appreciate the interest, and remind the caller of who initiated the contact.

Don't solicit customers before you leave. You might "sound out" a few trusted customers about what they might do if—hypothetically—you were to leave your present employment. However, this type of talk is dangerous and can be misunderstood. "Sounding out" may sound greedy to a judge. If you have a good product or service, it is better to proceed on the assumption that business will follow you. Indeed, given a choice, it is always better to create new business rather than take the old. If you do not hit your employer where it hurts, you are less likely to meet in the courts.

6
Lawyers And Lawsuits

It is no secret that lawyers are among the least trusted and liked of the professionals. This is no new development. Shakespeare wanted to kill them all. More's *Utopia* had no lawyers and the 1872 Constitution of the Illinois Grange offered membership to everyone except gamblers, actors, and lawyers.

Whether you view it as cause or effect, good or bad, the fact is that lawyers, judges, and litigation form the core of the system of protecting confidential information. You may or may not feel lawyers and judges are evil, but you cannot dispute that they are necessary. Knowing what your confidential information is and taking reasonable steps to protect it is essential, but you must understand how to fight for it.

This chapter presents a fox's view of chickenhouse architecture. We will examine the trade secret lawsuit, from the first warning letter to the settlement or trial, and consider what makes this type of litigation so interesting, fast-moving, and expensive. It covers what you should do if someone threatens or brings a lawsuit against you, and, if the shoe is on the other foot, what factors to consider before beginning litigation. Finally, with as much objectivity as possible, it describes how to choose and deal with your lawyer. No matter how good your case is, it will be shaped, controlled, and presented by someone else.

Trade Secrets Litigation

It is difficult to formulate consistent rules in trade secret or "unfair competition" litigation since each case depends so much on its particular facts. There is one major exception: they are all expensive. Litigation of any dispute has, unfortunately, become one of the costlier pursuits in today's society, and that is especially true of trade secret litigation. Often a great deal is at stake and plaintiffs will not hesitate to commit a wealth of resources to protect critical intellectual property. More importantly, these suits are often generated and sustained by an emotional reaction to the situation rather than a cold, objective analysis of the costs and potential benefits. Discovering that you may have been ripped off by some of your most trusted employees may provoke an automatic, immediate, and aggressive reaction of "get them, punish them, and forget about the cost." (Often the motivation is less pure. Left behind because things are not going well, the manager pursues litigation to create a scapegoat and divert attention from the department's shortcomings.) Finally, the issues are complex and usually require extensive fact investigation, far more than the ordinary contract case, for example.

Unfortunately litigation itself can be used as an anti-competitive tool. Established companies sometimes pursue a groundless lawsuit to destroy an incipient competitor. This is regrettable, and recent court rulings have permitted the targets of such litigation—when it is found to have been pursued solely for harassment—to sue the aggressors for their fees and damages. Most lawyers would not bring such a lawsuit. However, few cases are that simple; the totally meritless case is rare and the primary, but private motivation to squash the new competition can usually be hidden among more acceptable and supportable reasons for pursuing the case.

Using the unfair competition suit as a weapon against fledgling companies concerns those who organize and finance new businesses. Many venture capitalists will agree that in choosing between two otherwise equal opportunities they will avoid the start-up company with potential litigation problems. These people seek "positive" deals where management can focus undiverted attention on the new company's growth at the beginning, when its chance of failure is so high. Ill-equipped to judge the relative merits of litigation, potential investors are often scared away simply by a plaintiff's requests: not just money, but an injunction against manufacturing or shipping products, or employing particularly critical individuals. In one situation, a venture capitalist abandoned financing a new company simply because he was named as a "co-conspirator" in a trade secrets complaint.

The anti-competitive potential for abuse which is prevented by trade secret litigation is not easily resolved. The best advice for the targeted entrepreneur is to plan well, keep the lines of communication with the potential plaintiff open and be ready to respond quickly. As to the potential plaintiff: examine your motives carefully. In addition to the factors discussed later in this chapter, consider the ethical implications of employing litigation costs to bleed your competition to death. And finally, remember the sword has two edges; you may miscalculate the ability and determination of your adversary who may involve you in a much longer, more difficult, and expensive fight than you anticipate.

Another distinguishing feature of trade secret litigation is the inability to predict exactly what may happen until the facts are fully laid out in a courtroom. Again, it is the appearance of a fact rather than its existence which, together with surrounding, collateral facts, will determine the outcome of your suit. How the facts are perceived will vary among judges, and any single judge's perceptions may also vary substantially. In most jurisdictions, you will not know which judge will try your case until the first day of trial. And that may take a year or more. In the interim, you may be passed from judge to judge for pre-trial disputes.

Once you get to trial, a seemingly inconsequential fact may become critical or controlling as the judge attempts to "balance the equities" of the litigants' competing interests. In a case tried by a leading trade secrets lawyer in Texas, the defendant took a job with a competitor where his knowledge of the plaintiff's secret processes would surely be useful. The lawyer produced evidence of a study he had commissioned which concluded that at least several hundred jobs were available to the former employee around the country, in his area of work, where the former employer's trade secrets would not be compromised. The employee responded that his daughter's illness limited his choice of residence. If he could not work for that particular competitor, he would have to abandon his profession in order to stay in the area. The employee won.

Trade secret cases, although always expensive and sometimes frustrating, are nevertheless exciting. They have the human drama of a divorce without the depressing focus on personal trivia. Instead, they focus on the challenging issues of ownership rights to intellectual property and the ethics of business competition in a mobile society. Now, let's take a look at how they happen.

Anatomy of a Trade Secret Case

The typical case will not include all of these elements at once, but consider the following hypothetical situation.

Several employees, led by a former officer of the company, have left to form a competing business, selling a similar product to the same marketplace. The "leader" of the split-off group had lost an intra-corporate battle to define a new product. Management believes the new group may pursue those rejected concepts by building a product that employs other valuable and useful confidential information which the company wants to protect. In addition, because of the loyalty commanded by the departing officer, the company believes additional employees may be hired away, severely affecting certain ongoing product development projects. Finally, one of the employees who left was a middle-level manager in marketing and had recently participated in an extensive strategy planning session. Certain customers confide that they have been approached by the new group.

The company calls in its lawyers to prepare a complaint and request for injunction against use of its trade secrets, hiring its employees and soliciting its customers. The lawyers spend several days becoming familiar with the facts and the technology, securing sworn statements from company employees and other witnesses and preparing a sheaf of papers to begin court battle. Because of the shortness of time and a desire to keep the element of surprise, the company decides not to deliver a "demand letter" but to proceed with the court action.

At three o'clock one afternoon, the company's lawyers call the terminated officer (not knowing if he has yet retained a lawyer) and advise him that they will be in court at nine o'clock the next morning to request restraining orders. The officer—now for the first time a defendant in a lawsuit—frantically phones his lawyer. Fortunately, he had anticipated something like this and had previously consulted with his attorney about the problem. His lawyer calls the company's lawyer and manages to get copies of all the papers by five o'clock. Working into the wee hours with the client, the lawyer prepares for the hearing the next day, gathering as many facts and doing as much legal research as possible in the short time allowed. In the meantime, the new enterprise has come to a grinding halt, focusing its entire attention and energy on preparing defense.

The next morning, the judge takes 15 minutes before the regular calendar of cases to read over the papers and listen to both lawyers' arguments. The defense has not had time to prepare papers but the defense lawyer argues that the technology involved is not secret, the employees wanted to leave anyway, and the customers are easy to find, since they are listed in a trade directory he has brought with him. Nevertheless, the judge states that those factual issues are too involved to consider in detail at this stage. So, a temporary restraining order is issued as requested, simply to "maintain the status quo" until the facts can be thoroughly flushed out. The hearing—to determine whether the injunction should continue pending a full trial of the case—is set for two weeks later.

At this point, the new company receives the bad news. The lawyer needs at least $25,000 to take the case through the injunction hearing. Customers and suppliers have learned of the injunction (perhaps from the plaintiff) and will make no commitments and grant no credit until "everything is resolved." Financing opportunities dry up for the same reason, and the entrepreneurs spend all their time educating their lawyer and preparing for participating in depositions (question-and-answer sessions with the lawyers recorded by a court reporter) before the hearing. Worse, the lawyer confides it is possible that the court will continue the injunction, since the facts aren't stacking up as well as expected.

It is at this stage that most trade secret cases are won or lost. The judge will decide whether to grant a "preliminary injunction" pending a full trial on the merits of the case. If the order significantly impacts the business of the new company (and often *any* order because of its negative implications to the trade will have a severe impact), the defendant may come to terms, settling for less stringent restrictions, but which still tie his hands significantly and present the threat of a contempt proceeding if violated. At this stage the plaintiff may accept less than "full relief" just to get an order to justify the action and save the wounded corporate pride.

On the other hand, if the plaintiff loses the request for a preliminary injunction, there is little reason to proceed further with the case. The plaintiff will either abandon the case or accept a nominal settlement. The preliminary injunction hearing effectively becomes a "mini-trial" and significant effort is invested in preparing for it.

In our example, the preliminary injunction is issued and the former employer is flushed with victory. Nevertheless, the judge substantially watered down the order, and the new company's lawyers feel that it can proceed with the specific product on the boards without violating the order. Moreover, the judge has only prohibited them from "soliciting" employees and certain customers and has specifically granted the new venture the freedom to *accept* solicitations from them. Since its business has not been significantly impacted and the entire claim might be defeated at trial, clearing its good name, the defendant decides to continue its vigorous defense. In fact, the defendant decides that the best defense is a vigorous offense and files a cross-complaint against the plaintiff, alleging violations of the antitrust laws as well as other business claims, including trade defamation, interference with contractual relationships, and the like.

The defense asserts that the plaintiff has failed to take reasonable steps to protect its own trade secrets and is making its own working environment so miserable that its employees are encouraged to leave in droves, regardless of any solicitation from the defendant. In spite of its recent success, the plantiff may be wondering what it has really won. True, it has an order against the defendant, but loopholes abound and contempt of court by violating the injunction is difficult to prove. At the same time, it finds itself engaged in a public battle over the relative happiness of its staff and the true viability of its trade secrets, skirmishes that it may not want to fight over the long haul. And, of course, there is the bill for attorney fees, which really focuses the stark realities of litigation.

Now, the war of attrition begins, as each side girds itself for "discovery" from the other of facts supporting the many claims and defenses involved in the case. This discovery takes many forms. It includes depositions of employees from both sides, ranging from the chief executive officer to the documents file clerk. There will also be scores, or perhaps hundreds, of written questions to answer, and usually thousands of documents to produce. And the established company will have thousands or hundreds of thousands of relevant documents, while the defendant, a new company, will have only a few.

This activity engages the lawyers at great length, requires extensive management time and allows each side to comb through the other's most secret records. A "protective order" may be entered by the court, prohibiting each side from using information which it gleans from the discovery process for business purposes. However, many plaintiffs have expressed the justified fear that allowing this wide-ranging discovery permits the defendant to collect any details which the departing employees left behind. For this reason, sensitive data may be restricted to review by the lawyers, not the clients.

In this hypothetical case, each side uses the discovery process as a weapon. The defendant's lawyers tie up the plaintiff's remaining employees for several weeks, taking them from critical projects already postponed by the departure of their co-workers. And the plaintiff, bent on delivering a message if not simply putting the defendant out of business, takes the deposition of virtually all of the defendant's new and increasingly aggravated customers and suppliers. The law never intended this activity to arise from "discovery." These motivations may only be collateral to the legitimate goal of collecting facts necessary to develop a case or present a defense. Collateral or not, substantial interference with the business of the opposition is often a significant motive and almost always the result.

During this time, both sides engage highly paid consultants or experts. Their advice is sought regarding technological issues and customer list and employee raiding disputes. They document how easily an independent customer list can be created, the relative importance of price and other objective criteria in a particular market, and the ability of the plaintiff to have avoided all damage by hiring replacement personnel. Like psychiatrists at a criminal trial, experts in a trade secret case can offer wildly different opinions on the same issue. Nevertheless, because of the usually technical questions involved in such litigation, they are practically indispensable and a trade secret case rarely can be tried without them. Both sides in our hypothetical lawsuit require at least two experts, one dealing with issues of technology and the other an economist to testify as to the harm which was caused, or could have been avoided by each side.

The lawyers are not spending all of their time asking questions and looking at documents. They are in court, and quite often. This part of the case is called "motion practice," and indeed some of the motions that lawyers file suggest they are simply practicing. Trial lawyers are, by nature or training, combative and disagreeable types. They love argument, most of all their own. And trade secret cases offer numerous opportunities to demonstrate their contentiousness. This reflects both the desire to make the opponent spend money, and the complex and unusual issues which pervade these cases.

Attorneys go to court regularly to resolve interim disputes, including where the suit should be tried, what deposition questions should be answered, and whether a "special master" or court expert should be appointed. Each appearance generates more papers and demands more time and money. Significant aspects of the trial can be affected by these motions and results are often difficult to predict. Nevertheless, they take a lot of time, add to the fees, and lengthen the time before the trial.

When discovery and motion practice stops or slows substantially, both sides prepare for the ultimate conflict, the trial. Besides the preliminary injunction period, this is the stage when most trade secret litigation is settled. Both sides, including their attorneys, now understand what comprises their case and what the other side can do. A year or more has elapsed since the events which provoked the original complaint and the combatants now view their positions more objectively. Each faces huge costs at this juncture. Although the discovery and motion practice was expensive, it occurred over a longer period, permitting the legal fees to be paid in installments.

By contrast, trial preparation must be squeezed into approximately six weeks. Each lawyer advises the client that they face a time of extraordinary effort to gather, organize, and distill the massive information collected since the complaint was filed, to present it in a concise and logical format at trial. The fees for each week of this work will be huge, comparable only to the trial fees, which will immediately follow. Faced with the prospect of large cash outlays within a short time, the parties conclude that they have better things to do and reach an agreement.

In our hypothetical case, the plaintiff grants a non-exclusive license to the defendant enabling it to use the technology in return for a royalty. The plaintiff, now fully staffed, abandons its difficult-to-prove predatory hiring claim. The defendant throws the plaintiff a crumb by agreeing not to solicit additional employees and a few customers in which it had no interest anyway. All other claims are dropped. The settlement contract will remain confidential, permitting each side to imply to its employees and customers that it has won.

Our hypothetical case settled as most real ones do. But when such lawsuits do go to trial, they are among the more interesting and entertaining of commercial litigation. Imagine a judge or jury, not a technical degree among them, trying to understand and evaluate the relationship between two semiconductor designs or complex chemical processes. Or a plaintiff company fighting over the "theft" of an "invaluable" lower-level employee who had consistently gotten bad reviews and small raises. Or imagine both sides, fiercely arguing over each other's product and marketing plans, turning around to see representatives from several of their mutual competitors sitting in the audience. Consider these scenarios when threatened with a trade secret lawsuit or contemplating bringing one yourself.

You Might Be Sued

If you skipped Chapter 4, read it now to learn how to avoid getting sued by your former employer. If you employ someone who has just left a competitor, review that information with your new hire. If those suggestions have generally been followed, you probably will not be sued at all. Remember your potential adversary is run by businessmen whose ultimate concern is to increase profits, not wage legal wars. They will not come after you so long as they believe you have not threatened their business, or antagonized them by making them feel that they have been ripped off.

Never "defame" the former employer in the marketplace. A less-than-friendly parting and the new entrepreneur's heady feelings of independence and power, encourage an irresistible temptation to take shots at the old place. If nothing else, it helps justify the decision to yourself. Don't do it. Not only do you risk waking a sleeping giant, but you gain nothing from the disparagement. In fact, your trade relationships may improve when your customers realize that your business reflects your superiority, rather than your perception of the inferiority of others.

If your former employer sends a "warning letter" (see Appendix B), don't panic. Frequently, companies automatically send such a letter to every departing employee. Of course, if your situation is unusual, and real, meaningful threats challenge your ability to pursue your occupation, or directly accuse you of theft, immediately get legal counsel. On the other hand, the "form" warning letter deserves a "form" response.

Dear Company Lawyer:

Thank you for your recent letter. Please don't be concerned because although I don't necessarily agree with everything you said, I certainly intend to meet all my obligations to the company.

However, it never has been explained to me exactly what are the "trade secrets" and "proprietary information" you claim to own. I know you don't mean to say that I can't continue to work in my field; but I want to be sure there's no misunderstanding. If you would be so kind as to describe precisely what it is that you claim as your trade secrets, then I will be able to make a better judgment about it.

I'm sure I don't have any documents that are sensitive. I was very careful to leave everything at the company except my personal papers. If you would like to examine them to satisfy your concerns, please give me a call.

Finally, let me emphasize that I want to continue to do everything I can to make the transition smooth. If anything comes up where I might be of assistance, please don't hesitate to contact me.

Very truly yours,

Former employee

The first paragraph of this letter constitutes a form of "estoppel letter," discussed briefly in Chapter 4. It challenges the company to *define* its trade secrets, a challenge it will probably not accept. If the company remains silent, it will find it much harder to later obtain any court orders prohibiting your use of its proprietary information. The remainder of the letter creates a record that you present no threat and do not intend to harm the company. The judge who considers this evidence, even though it is self-serving, may be less likely to issue an injunction.

Document Your Intentions. This is your chance to create your record. If you are sued, you will be more likely to win and win quickly and cheaply. If you suspect a claim of technology theft, make sure you have no plans, specifications, drawings, or other documents belonging to your former employer.

From the outset of your organizational efforts, record how you create or acquire *your own* technology. Don't delay this effort until you have more time, since an after-the-fact record is virtually useless. It is paramount to immediately create written records regarding customer list development. To defeat a customer list claim, you must demonstrate that from day one you worked feverishly to create your list from publicly available sources and pursued that information. To defend a claim of employee raiding, be prepared with minutes of your interviews, which show that each employee solicited the new employment, provided information concerning compensation and benefits, and confirmed in writing that obligations to the former employer have not been violated (see Appendix F).

Everyone who enjoys television or the movies knows whatever you say to the police can and will be held against you. The same applies to what you say from the time you leave your former employer until a lawsuit is filed, and for sometime thereafter. Whatever you say to anyone—customers, your new employer, employees who left, employees who stayed, suppliers, friends, and so on—can be "discovered" by the other side in a lawsuit. Litigation is like living in a goldfish bowl. You can be asked about every conversation or communication you've had with anyone. Only communications with your lawyer and sometimes your spouse are fully protected from disclosure. Therefore, you can do a lot for yourself at this stage simply by keeping your mouth shut. When you must talk, consider how your statement might appear, if taken out of context, or after passed among several persons. Prepare a story concerning the circumstances of the split-off for customers.

Emphasize your lack of ill will and your desire to proceed fairly. It may sound cute at the time, but if your customers think so, they'll remember it. If they are ever asked to testify, the effect can be extremely helpful.

Above all, if any serious possibility of litigation exists, consult a qualified lawyer at the earliest possible time. Relatively little preparation can pay off enormously if a lawsuit later develops, or even by avoiding a lawsuit that otherwise would have been filed. And remember, securing legal consulting services to avoid litigation costs a fraction of the legal fees required to defend a lawsuit.

You Want to Sue

If you still seriously think about litigation after reading this far, then you probably have been seriously wronged. Many trade secret attorneys spend a great deal of time trying to convince their clients not to sue. Nevertheless, many clients pursue litigation in spite of the best advice, and, of course, many ought to sue because the circumstances justify it. But before you make that difficult decision, marshall your forces.

Document Your Case. Consider first what evidence will demonstrate the defendant's actions. The physical evidence may include documents, missing equipment, and the like. Identify and secure the evidence immediately. Create records of the events; maintain a log of names, times, and events as they occur. (Address this log to your attorney so that its contents will be privileged from discovery.) In a separate file, document all the damage you've suffered as a result of the defendant's conduct. Some damage such as the threatened loss of trade secret protection by publication to the outside world can be deemed "irreparable" with specific descriptions of the possible loss. This will often be enough to get an injunction. Money damages such as a lost account or extra training or redesign costs can be recovered, but only if sufficiently documented.

Identify which employees will remain loyal and which may be targets for further attack by your competitors (or, indeed, may already be committed to leaving). Interview anyone knowing about events relevant to the litigation. Besides preserving the facts before recollections fade and providing an objective source of facts to help you decide whether to litigate, these interviews offer other advantages. Loyal employees may be strengthened in their commitment by participating in the exposure of the bad guys. At the least, they will be impressed with your seriousness and be unlikely to consider actions invoking your wrath. Secretly disloyal employees may be exposed through the attitude they demonstrate when asked to cooperate in the investigation.

Contact your suppliers when appropriate to learn whether your new competition has requested any parts or supplies revealing the development stage of a competitive product (or whether it employs any of your proprietary data). Customers too, should be discreetly polled for information regarding the mutineers' timing and content of marketing contacts. Although risky, this may have a preventative effect, encouraging customers to carefully consider shifting their loyalties.

Finally, consider hiring a private investigator to determine your competitor's activities. This approach provides advantages of secrecy, objectivity, and professionalism. However, proceed cautiously. The skills and abilities of investigators vary and few are sufficiently experienced in trade secret cases. Further, with private investigators, you always run the risk of an invasion of privacy claim. Whatever might be the real merits and potential exposure to you, such a claim can drastically affect the judge or jury's perception of you in litigation. And again, the side which appears more righteous and noble will prevail, regardless of the "hard facts."

Consult an experienced, qualified lawyer as soon as possible. With every day that passes without counsel, evidence may be dissipated and you may miss critical opportunities to take action. The courts have stressed that plaintiffs should bring claims early before the defendant has proceeded very far with the new enterprise. The more commitments made, the more money spent, and the more the defendant's position has changed before you serve notice, the less likely you can obtain useful relief from the courts.

Often the notice you serve consists simply of a "warning letter" addressed to the departed employee and perhaps to the new employer. A carefully drafted and properly timed letter can serve your purposes perfectly, without resorting to a lawsuit. However, to avoid any misunderstandings and to take full advantage of this opportunity, draft such a letter with legal counsel, and carefully tailor it to the facts of the situation. (See Appendix B; like the other Appendices' forms, however, it is only an example, and should only be used in consultation with qualified counsel.)

Suppose the "friendly" approach doesn't work and you must make the tough decision whether to cross the Rubicon and file a lawsuit. Sometimes you have no choice, as when your obligation as a licensee compels you to pursue those who might compromise the integrity of licensed proprietary technology. However, most of the time you should carefully weigh a number of factors before jumping into the fray.

Consider Litigation Critically. Closely and realistically examine your objectives. What have you really lost? Are you looking for a settlement? You must assume that your case will go to trial and take a great deal of time and money. You may not be able to get the "immediate relief" you believe is available by simply threatening or filing a lawsuit. Nevertheless, an early settlement is sometimes possible and you must carefully calculate what each side has to gain and lose from the litigation. If your objective is to "send a message" to the departed employees, their new employer, or your current employees, consider whether this is the most effective or efficient way to send such a message.

On the other hand, taking a consistently aggressive stand to protect yourself will create a reputation that is an extremely useful deterrent to potential unfair competition. If you never sue, you may be considered a patsy, and a supplier of key employees to highly competitive start-ups. If your goal is to *stop* the defendants, carefully consider your chances of securing injunctive relief, how strong the real impact of such an order would be, and whether it can be realistically enforced in a way that is valuable to you.

If your objective is to recover damages, seriously consider the ability of the other side to pay any judgment, and the length of time that it takes to collect in your jurisdiction. Finally, if you really wish to eliminate your new competition, carefully consider not only the legality and ethics of such an approach but also the cost effectiveness. Although your competition may have to match each dollar you spend in pursuing a lawsuit, that is not always the case. Many experienced managers believe that given an equal commitment of time and resources, a new competitor is more likely to be beaten in the marketplace than in the courtroom.

Ponder carefully the costs incurred for the privilege of pursuing your lawsuit. You can expect to pay anywhere from $100,000 in attorney's fees before it is all over. In a heavily documented case, the copying bills alone can run $5000 per month. Additional fees for consultants and expert witnesses, transcripts, travel expenses, and so on, may have a significant impact on your budget. But not only money is involved; for many plaintiffs the greater sacrifice is in lost time of management and staff. Depositions, researching files, consultation with lawyers, etc. take time from regular duties. Concentration and energy is diverted from everyday duties and goals in favor of the lawsuit. This factor is often overlooked by the naive, but can significantly affect an ongoing business.

Weigh objectively the potential benefits from the litigation as they relate to your own staff. Remember, the deterrent effect of potential litigation may curtail further raiding. Once a suit is filed, you can't do more. But if you don't sue, you may be considered an "easy touch" and encourage further predatory activity by your current and future employees and competitors. In addition, you can positively affect employee morale from this type of litigation, if properly pursued, and if employees are kept advised of the reasons for, and the progress of, the lawsuit. In many situations, the departing employees were widely disliked by their co-workers, who will expect and be gratified by an employer's aggressive action. However, their friends may think you're picking on the little guys, practicing slavery, or otherwise interfering with their freedom.

Consider the risks inherent in proceeding with the litigation. Filing a complaint may not bring the competition to its knees or even to the bargaining table. Instead, the defendant may file a cross-complaint against you for antitrust claims, trade libel, other business torts, or for a declaration of invalidity of your patents. Moreover, do not ignore the potentially negative effect of litigation upon your customers and suppliers, who may find themselves dragged into court for depositions, or even named in the lawsuit themselves. This involuntary involvement may invoke a response of "plague on both your houses" and the customer will take its business elsewhere.

Finally, prepare for the worst, and consider the effects of losing the case. Far from creating an effective deterrent, you may ultimately be perceived as a paper tiger. Perhaps more importantly, this lawsuit becomes the forum for testing your trade secrets and you are playing your trump card. If proved wrong, you will not only have failed in this case, but also in many later challenges of your ability to protect your trade secrets.

Proceed with a Plan. If you decide to go forward, a number of preliminary questions should be discussed with your counsel. The first is in which court to bring the suit. Federal and state courts vary substantially in the time it takes to go to trial, the reliability of the judges, the breadth of discovery that is allowed, and other procedural factors.

Consider also who to name as defendants. When a competitor hires a former employee, one school of thought advises bringing a suit only against the employee, since the new employer may cut the employee off when it has not yet been directly involved. (Indeed, if it is not named directly, the new employer may not even provide the employee with legal counsel.) An injunction against an employee "and all those who act in concert with him" affects the new employer as if it had been named specifically.

Finally, determine whether to request an injunction with incomplete evidence at the beginning, when that kind of relief matters most, or to wait until later in the litigation when you have gathered more facts through the discovery process. It is quite demoralizing to the plaintiff to fail in an application for a preliminary injunction.

After you have committed yourself to a program, proceed quickly. In the early stages, your new competitor, like the animal that has just shed its skin, is most vulnerable. The defendant will better appreciate the seriousness of your position when you pursue it immediately after realizing the harm. Most importantly, if effective in an early stage, you will have stopped the outward flow of trade secrets, employees, and business before more serious damage occurs. However, unless you find a "smoking gun" (for example, stolen documents), you may have no case until the new venture develops enough to make use of your trade secrets.

Inform your employees of the progress of litigation but be careful how you do it. They must be aware but not intimidated. Be sensitive to spies within your ranks who might be waiting for a signal to leave, and who are feeding information to the other side in the interim.

Always keep your sights on a possible trial of the case and don't develop an expectation of an early settlement. Nevertheless, be ready at any stage of the proceeding to objectively assess your position and compromise your objectives. After all, you are running a business, not engaging in a duel.

Tell your attorney everything, and insist that he or she tell you everything. Obtain copies of everything that is filed with the court and all other paperwork generated during the progress of the case. Insist that your attorney provide you with periodic estimates, bills, reports, planning sessions, and debriefing. Don't be afraid to ask questions. At the least, get an education; you certainly don't want to go through this again.

Choosing a Lawyer

Many lawyers are egocentric, insufferable people. They are usually taught at law school to be narrow minded and to speak among themselves in a language that no one else can understand. Clearly these things can be said of other professionals, but lawyers, because of their pervasive influence in business and government, are especially targeted for criticism. However, in the area of trade secrets, lawyers—and especially trial lawyers—are indispensable. Like it or not, planning to protect and defend your proprietary information requires legal assistance.

Search for Trust

Whether you have been sued, are thinking of suing, or are simply devising a plan to protect your trade secrets, you need to choose a lawyer. What do you look for? In a word, trust. How can you trust people you don't like? A good question, but try it. In spite of their reputation, many lawyers are fine people. You might not want to be friends with them, but you should be able to find one that you feel confident with. To find someone who gives you that comfort, you should interview as extensively as possible.

Start your search as soon as possible. Your choice may be limited, as when you are served with papers requiring you to appear the next day at a hearing. Fortunately that circumstance is relatively infrequent. Normally you can arrange enough time for interviewing. Remember, when you buy tickets five minutes before the show, you pay a high price and get a bad seat.

Create a list of lawyers who have both a good reputation and experience in trade secret litigation. Although not a recognized specialty in some states, most lawyers will recognize trade secret law and know whether they or their colleagues are sufficiently experienced. "Unfair competition" is also a phrase which refers to this specialty. If you cannot find someone with that specific expertise, look for an excellent trial lawyer. Many handle a variety of disputes, and the trial lawyer's skills and abilities are far more important than technical knowledge in a trade secret dispute.

Check out a lawyer's experience level in advance by consulting "law lists" found at local public or law libraries (such as the *Martindale-Hubbel* volumes which cover lawyers throughout the United States). These resources will also provide information about the size of a firm, the type of practice it engages in, and often a representative sampling of its clients. As to reputation, you must ask people who have had a similar or related matter satisfactorily handled by a lawyer. Avoid the generalist who practices alone, or lawyers in totally unrelated specialties, unless they can verify the reputations of possible candidates you have identified. Trade associations are another referral source.

If you seek patent or copyright protection for your intellectual property, then your choice is clear. Many firms in most metropolitan areas of the country specialize in patent, trademark, and copyright law. Because of the close relationship between that specialized practice and the area of trade secret protection and unfair competition, these lawyers can often provide excellent advice on these subjects as well, or can refer you to the lawyers who can. Remember, significant trial lawyer experience is essential in trade secret litigation.

Most lawyers do not practice alone, but in law firms, which range in size from two to two hundred or more lawyers. Remember, you want one or two individuals with whom you can establish a relationship of trust and confidence. In achieving that goal, it doesn't matter whether you select one from a small or large firm. Smaller firms usually have more efficient practices and provide a closer, personal, contact between lawyer and client. Large firms often "over-lawyer" a case by involving too many associates. You may not want to pay for their training. Nevertheless, certain types of matters are better handled by the larger firms, and some of the best specialists can be found there.

Consider Fees

Whoever you choose, be openly concerned about budgeting. Find out how your lawyer will charge you. Arrangements vary, but usually one of these three types is offered:

- An hourly fee; the amount you pay depends on the time the lawyer spends on your matter.
- A contingent fee; the lawyer is paid only if money is recovered.

- A value-determined fee; several subjective factors reflect the value of the service rendered.

The contingent fee is extremely unusual in trade secret litigation, primarily because the plaintiff seeks primarily an injunction, rather than damages. I strongly favor the "reasonable value" approach. If a relationship of trust and reasonably good communication exists between you and your lawyer, you probably will not be hurt by this method. On the other hand, paying by the hour promotes sloth, rewards inefficiency, and encourages "running the meter," regardless of the usefulness of the activity involved.

Discuss the fee arrangement at the beginning of the relationship. Be frank and demand candid answers to your budgeting concerns. Firm quotes are impossible, but get an estimate of expected fees and costs, even if it's only a range. Learn how much of the work on a lawsuit you can do to save the time of your lawyer and staff. Most lawyers welcome this cooperative effort and it could provide substantial savings. You can be specifically involved in researching facts, gathering and organizing documents, and preparing written responses to discovery requests. Finally, when you have agreed with your lawyer about the fee arrangement and the scope of work to be accomplished, get it in writing. That suggestion is not inconsistent with the requirement of trust in the relationship, but simply helps avoid misunderstandings as the project progresses.

You and your lawyer must have good regular communication. Insist on regular progress reports and periodic strategy conferences. Most lawyers carry large case loads, and regular contact concerning your case will make your lawyer more efficient in serving you. On the other hand, don't be on the phone with every question that pops into your head; save your questions for these conferences, when they can be more efficiently covered at the same time.

Above all, don't be intimidated by your lawyer. Although you should respect your counsel's judgment and rely on decisions made on your behalf, you are entitled to understand each step of the project or lawsuit. If you feel you aren't being adequately informed, inform your lawyer and insist that the relationship change or be terminated. Treat your lawyer as a trusted guide and adviser; but do not be cut out of the process. Only when you continually understand what is going on can you make intelligent decisions about allocating resources for the next step.

Appendices

The idea that intellectual property is a real but often overlooked business asset is the central theme of this book. To that premise, I add the undisputed assumption that the protagonists in trade secret disputes would do better by staying out of these legal battles. Finally, to avoid the apparently unavoidable fight you must prepare to win it. The employer's process is simply stated: first, identify your proprietary information; second, create a continuing system for classifying and protecting it; and third, act swiftly and decisively when its integrity is threatened. For employees who want to capitalize on their own ideas the process is: first, clarify what is yours and what isn't; second, carefully plan your new activity to minimize the perceived threat to your employer; and finally, execute your plans in a professional, deliberate fashion.

Whatever your perspective, remember everything you do is in preparation for a possible lawsuit. No matter how good your intentions are, appearances control the outcome. And written records define those appearances. To help you create those records properly, I have presented several forms which are frequently used in my practice. Although I recommend them for your review and reference, I emphasize again that applicable law varies among jurisdictions and is subject to change. Therefore, rely on your attorney's advice before using any of them.

A

CONFIDENTIALITY AGREEMENT FOR A POTENTIAL PARTNER OR JOINT VENTURER

_______________ (hereafter "Inventor" [or "Discloser" or your name]) and _______________ (hereafter "Disclosee") wish to consider the possibility of a joint venture relating to _______________ (for example, a process or manufacture of an item). It is therefore necessary and desirable that Disclosee have access to certain information relating to the _______________ . This information constitutes a trade secret of Inventor, and is disclosed only for this purpose. Disclosee agrees to preserve in confidence such information, and not to use it for any other purpose. Disclosee shall obtain, from each of its employees and agents which it designates to have access to this information, an acknowledgment that such employee or agent has read and agrees to be bound by this agreement.

On termination of the joint venture or of the negotiations which gave rise to this agreement, Disclosee shall promptly return all materials containing such information, including all extracts and copies thereof, to Inventor.

This agreement shall not apply to information in the public domain at the time of disclosure, to information lawfully in the possession of Disclosee immediately prior to disclosure, or to information thereafter lawfully obtained by Disclosee from third parties.

B

LETTER TO DEPARTED EMPLOYEE

Dear Former Employee:

Since you have recently terminated your employment, we wish to remind you of your obligations to the company which continue after your employment ends. As you know, the company possesses a great deal of confidential business information and proprietary technology. This includes customer lists, marketing plans, engineering data, product plans, and the like. During your employment, you have been provided, or had access to, such information.

Both the law and the contract you signed when you came to work for the company prohibit any use or disclosure of such information after you leave. For your convenience, we are enclosing a copy of the agreement you signed. Because you have taken employment with a competitor of the company, it is especially important that you take care not to violate your obligations to keep this information confidential. The company considers it to be very important property, and will not hesitate to take any legal action necessary to protect it.

We hope that such action will not be necessary in your case, and that you will respect the trust and confidence which we have had in you as an employee. If you have any doubts or questions about the specifics of your continuing obligations to us, please do not hesitate to contact me.

Very truly yours,

In this letter, the description of the proprietary information is purposefully vague. Presumably, the employee will know fairly well what you mean. If the employee takes the unusual step of contacting you for clarification, then you certainly should arrange a time to meet and discuss the letter, specifying those matters which the employee has been exposed to (and be sure to document it with a follow-up letter). On the other hand, if he does not reply, a judge would probably infer that the employee understood very well what the obligations were.

C

LETTER TO NEW EMPLOYER OF DEPARTED EMPLOYEE

Gentlemen:

We understand that Mr. Smith, who until recently was employed by us, has decided to join your firm. We would like to draw your attention to the fact that Mr. Smith worked in our ______________________ department as a ______________ . In that capacity, he became quite familar with our ______________ process, which we consider and treat as confidential and proprietary.

In connection with his employment, Mr. Smith signed a Proprietary Information and Invention Agreement, a copy of which we are enclosing for your reference. We have no doubt that Mr. Smith intends to comply with his obligations and respect our trade secrets in this area. We also trust that your company will not assign Mr. Smith to a position in which he might consciously or inadvertently disclose or use any of our trade secrets.

If you have any questions regarding any of these matters, we will be happy to clarify them for you. We would appreciate your confirmation of your intent to ensure that Mr. Smith will not be called upon to violate any of his obligations to us.

May we please have your reply.

Very truly yours,

In using this form, it is necessary to be more specific about the type of sensitive information to which the employee has been exposed, since it cannot be presumed that the new employer will be familiar with it. Also, be careful what you say here. Any false and derogatory statements could create a defamation claim for the employee, which could be effectively used to blunt a legitimate effort by you to protect your trade secrets. And some states impose civil and criminal penalties on misstatements to new employers.

D

EMPLOYEE INSTRUCTIONS REGARDING THE EMPLOYER'S PROPRIETARY INFORMATION

Company business must not be discussed off premises.

Visitors to the company must be escorted at all times. Visitors must sign in and out at the front entrance, and be escorted by a Company employee while they are in the facilities. Take care not to allow access to areas which are off-limits to visitors. If you are not sure which areas are acceptable, please contact ______________ .

Documents which might contain proprietary information must be stamped "CONFIDENTIAL." All department managers have a set of written procedures describing the type of proprietary information likely to be generated within their departments. Be familiar with these procedures and follow them carefully. Generally, any document which contains internal product data, engineering data, or marketing information should be plainly marked with the rubber stamps which have been distributed. All personnel documents should be classified this way. If you have any doubt as to whether a document should be stamped, you should stamp it. Documents which are stamped should never leave the premises, except under specific arrangement with your supervisor. Photocopies should be limited to the number necessary for distribution. When a working copy is no longer needed, it should be destroyed. Remember the overall objective: we want to identify all our proprietary information and keep it within the Company.

Company equipment must not be taken from the premises without written authorization. Although certain employees may find it convenient to do some work at home, this must be done only with the specific and continuing approval of your supervisor. It is the employee's responsibility to account for Company equipment and materials at all times.

Employee publications and speeches on technical matters must first be submitted for review. Certain employees may have the opportunity to present papers or publish articles or books in their area of technical expertise. The Company encourages this. However, in order to be sure that proprietary technical data or product plans are not inadvertently disclosed, all such materials must be provided in advance to your supervisor for review. If there is any disagreement concerning what should or should not be included, you are assured that the matter will be thoroughly discussed with you and upper management.

All agreements and purchase orders that might involve use or disclosure of proprietary information must be reviewed and approved by your department manager.

PROPRIETARY TECHNICAL AND BUSINESS INFORMATION

What Is It?

The Company develops information which it uses in its business. This information may relate to technical matters, such as the development of a new product or service, or to non-technical matters, such as marketing information. All of this belongs to the Company, and together constitutes a very valuable and important asset, much like our buildings, fixtures, and inventory.

Examples of proprietary information (also called "trade secrets") include inventions, formulas, processes, new business ideas, customer information, marketing plans, and sales forecasts [you may want to add more specific categories peculiar to your business]. These are just examples, of course, and the Company's proprietary information includes many more specific items than are listed here.

Proprietary information will often be in writing. But even if it is not, it still is important Company property. An idea or customer data which is "in a person's head" is just as entitled to protection from misuse or disclosure to others.

If you ever have any questions concerning what qualifies as proprietary information, or whether a particular document or piece of information is company property, please see ______________.

Why Is It Important?

Ours is not the only business in this field. We face very stiff competition for the goods and services we sell. If we are to remain in business, we must protect and use all our assets wisely, because that is what our competitors do.

Any particular item of proprietary information gives us an "edge" over our competition. But it only remains useful if we know what it is and they don't. Therefore, it is very important that proprietary documents and data stay strictly within the Company.

What Is Your Role In Protecting It?

Studies show that most loss of proprietary data occurs not through deliberate theft or industrial espionage, but simply because of employee carelessness. In another section of this handbook [or in a separate flyer concerning procedures] we have described the "regulations" and procedures which are necessary for protecting our trade secrets. *Your personal attention to following these rules may make the difference.* Do not create exceptions because it seems easier or more convenient at the time.

From time to time, we will issue and post bulletins regarding steps which you should follow on particular matters. Please note these carefully.

If you ever observe any violation of the Company's procedures or notice anything which makes you suspect a possible breach of security, please report it immediately to your management.

If your employment with the Company terminates for any reason, remember your obligation to return all materials and equipment. In addition, do not forget that your obligation to protect the Company's proprietary information continues after you leave.

With the cooperation of everyone who works with proprietary information, we will be able to utilize this very important asset to increase the Company's success. This will benefit all of us.

E

CONFIDENTIAL DISCLOSURE AGREEMENT FOR PROSPECTIVE LICENSEE

Prospective Licensee

[Address]

re: [technology or idea]

Gentlemen:
We understand that you wish to receive information about the above [e.g., invention] in order to evaluate your interest in acquiring a license to use it. We are willing to disclose this information to you, which includes proprietary information we consider to be confidential and valuable, provided that you agree to the following terms:

1. "Confidential Information" shall mean proprietary technical information relating to the invention which is disclosed to you by us (or on our behalf), either directly or indirectly, in writing or by drawings or by inspection of facilities or in any other way. It is understood that Confidential Information shall not include:
   (a) Information which was in the public domain at the time of disclosure or,
   (b) Information which was in your possession prior to the time of its disclosure hereunder, or
   (c) Information which, though originally Confidential Information, subsequently becomes part of the public knowledge or literature through no fault of yours, as of the date of its becoming part of the public knowledge or literature, or
   (d) Information which, though originally Confidential Information, subsequently is received by you without obligations of secrecy from a third party who is free to disclose the information, as of the date of such third-party disclosure, or
   (e) Information independently developed by your employees or agents who you can show have had no access to Confidential Information received hereunder.

   Confidential Information disclosed under this Agreement

2. You agree that you will not disclose Confidential Information received hereunder to any third party without our prior written consent.
3. You agree that you will not make any commercial use of Confidential Information received hereunder except as may be provided for in separate agreements.
4. You agree that Confidential Information received hereunder will be treated with the same care that you use in the protection of your own proprietry information and will be disclosed only to those of your employees needed to evaluate and use it for the purpose noted above. You will advise each employee who is necessarily given access to such information of its confidential nature and the existence and importance of this Agreement.
5. This Confidential Disclosure Agreement shall not be construed to grant you any license or other rights except as provided herein.

If the foregoing is acceptable to your, please have this Agreement signed and dated by an appropriate officer of your company and return one fully executed copy to us.

Very truly yours,

Potential Licensor

By ______________________

Accepted and Agreed to this

________ *day of* __________, *19* _______.

Potential Licensee

By ____________________

Title ____________________

F

PROPRIETARY INFORMATION AND EMPLOYEE INVENTIONS AGREEMENT

IT IS AGREED BETWEEN ____________, hereinafter "the Company") and __________ (hereinafter "Employee") as follows:

1. Employment

The Company has hired Employee to work in the position of ____________. This employment is not for any particular period, and may be terminated, with or without cause, at any time. Employee acknowledges that, as a part of his/her employment, he/she is expected to create inventions and/or ideas of value to the Company.

2. Confidential Information of Others

Employee does not have in his/her possession any confidential information or documents belonging to others, and will not use, disclose to the Company, or induce the Company to use, any such information or documents during his/her employment. Employee represents that his/her employment will not require him/her to violate any obligation to or confidence with another.

3. Definition of Subsidiary

As used herein, the term "Subsidiary" means any corporation in which not less than 50% of the outstanding capital stock having voting power to elect a majority of its Board of Directors is owned, directly or indirectly, by the Company.

4. Definition of Proprietary Information

As used herein, the term "Proprietary Information" refers to any and all information of a confidential, proprietary, or secret nature which is or may be either applicable to, or related in any way to (i) the business, present or future, of the Company or any Subsidiary, (ii) the research and development or investigations of the Company or any Subsidiary, or (iii) the business of any customer of the Company or of any Subsidiary. Proprietary Information includes, for example and without limitation, trade secrets, processes, formulas, data, know-how, improvements, inventions, techniques, marketing plans and strategies, and information concerning customers or vendors.

5. Proprietary Information to be Kept in Confidence

Employee acknowledges that the Proprietary Information is a special, valuable, and unique asset of the Company, and Employee agrees at all times during the period of his/her employment and therefter to keep in confidence and trust all Proprietary Information. Employee agrees that during the period of his/her employment and thereafter he/she will not directly or indirectly use the Proprietary Information other than in the course of performing duties as an employee of the Company, nor will Employee directly or indirectly disclose any Proprietary Information or anything relating thereto to any person or entity, except in the course of performing duties as an employee of the Company and with the consent of the Company. Employee will abide by the Company's policies and regulations, as established from time to time, for the protection of its Proprietary Information.

6. **Other Employment**

Employee agrees that during the period of his/her employment by the Company, he/she will not, without the Company's prior written consent, directly or indirectly engage in any employment, consulting, or activity other than for the Company relating to any line of business in which the Company is now or at such time is engaged, or which would otherwise conflict with his/her employment obligations to the Company.

7. Return of Materials at Termination

In the event of any termination of his/her employment, whether or not for cause and whatever the reason, Employee will promptly deliver to the Company, or any Subsidiary designated by it, all documents, data, records, and other information pertaining to his/her employment, and Employee shall not take any documents or data, or any reproduction or excerpt of any documents or data, containing or pertaining to any Proprietary Information.

8. Disclosure to Company; Inventions as Sole Property of Company

Employee agrees promptly to disclose to the Company any and all inventions, discoveries, improvements, trade secrets, formulas, techniques, processes, and know-how, whether or not patentable and whether or not reduced to practice, conceived or learned by employee during the period of his/her employment, either alone or jointly with others, which relate to or result from the actual or anticipated business, work, research, or investigations of the Company or any Subsidiary, or which result, to any extent, from use of the Company's premises or property (the work being hereinafter collectively referred to as the "Inventions").

Employee acknowledges and agrees that all the Inventions shall be the sole property of the Company or any other entity designated by it, and the Employee hereby assigns to the Company his/her entire right and interest in all the Inventions; provided, however, that such assignment does not apply to any Invention which qualifies fully under the provisions of Section 2870 of the California Labor Code. The Company or any other entity designated by it shall be the sole owner of all domestic and foreign rights pertaining to the Inventions. Employee further agrees as to all the Inventions to assist the Company in every way (at the Company's expense) to obtain and from time to time enforce patents on the Inventions in any and all countries. To that end, by way of illustration but not limitation, Employee will testify in any suit or other proceeding involving any of the Inventions, execute all documents which the Company reasonably determines to be necessary or convenient for use in applying for and obtaining patents thereon and enforcing same, and execute all necessary assignments thereof to the Company or persons designated by it. Employee's obligation to assist the Company in obtaining and enforcing patents for the Inventions shall continue beyond the termination of his/her employment, but the Company shall compensate Employee at a reasonable rate after such termination for time actually spent by Employee at the Company's request on such assistance.

9. List of Prior Inventions

All inventions, if any, which Employee made prior to employment by the Company are excluded from the scope of this Agreement. As a matter of record, Employee has set forth on Exhibit A attached hereto a complete list of all inventions, discoveries, or improvements relating to the Company's business which have been made by Employee prior to his/her employment with the Company. Employee represents and covenants that such list is complete.

10. Injunction

Employee agrees that it would be difficult to measure damage to the Company from any breach by Employee of the promises set forth in Paragraphs 5, 6, 7, and 8 herein, that injury to the Company from any such breach would be impossible to calculate, and that money damages would therefore be an inadequate remedy for any such breach. Accordingly, Employee agrees that if he/she shall breach any provision of Paragraphs 5, 6, 7, or 8, the Company shall be entitled, in addition to all other remedies it may have, to injunctions or other appropriate orders to restrain any such breach by employee without showing or proving any actual damage sustained by the Company.

11. General

(a) To the extent that any of the agreements set forth herein, or any word, phrase, clause, or sentence thereof, shall be found to be illegal or unenforceable for any reason, such agreement, word, clause, phrase, or sentence shall be modified or deleted in such a manner so as to make the agreement as modified legal and enforceable under applicable laws, and the balance of the agreements or parts thereof shall not be affected thereby, the balance being construed as severable and independent.

(b) This Agreement shall be binding upon Employee and his/her heirs, executors, assigns, and administrators and shall inure to the benefit of the Company, its successors and assigns, and any Subsidiary.

(c) This Agreement shall be governed by the laws of the State of California, which state shall have jurisdiction of the subject matter hereof.

(d) This Agreement may be signed in two counterparts, each of which shall be deemed an original and which together shall constitute one instrument.

(e) The use of the singular in this Agreement includes the plural, as appropriate.

(f) This Agreement represents the entire agreement between Employee and the Company with respect the the subject matter hereof, superseding all previous oral or written communications, representations, or agreements. This Agreement may be modified only by a duly authorized and executed writing.

	EMPLOYEE:
Dated: ______________________	Dated: ______________________
______________________	______________________ Signature
By: ______________________	______________________ Typed or Printed Name

CAUTION TO EMPLOYEE: This Agreement affects important rights. DO NOT sign it unless you have read it carefully, and are satisfied that you understand it completely.

G
NONCOMPETITION COVENANTS

Covenants not to compete are not always enforced precisely according to their terms, since most courts are reluctant to interfere with an individual's right to earn a livelihood. Indeed, in some states (for example, California and Michigan), a direct noncompetition covenant may be completely void. Therefore, you and your counsel should carefully consider the various alternatives set forth here (or some variant of them). Remember the overriding principle that post-employment restrictions must be "reasonable" in specifying time and geography. In fact, consider using more than one clause, applying each less restrictive provision only in the event that the prior one is held invalid (this approach is subject to criticism; it may give the employee the false impression that a particular clause is unenforceable, substantially lessening the deterrent effect of the agreement).

Straight Noncompete

> "Employee agrees that for a period of ____ years after termination of employment, he/she will not compete, directly or indirectly, with the Company in any of its business. Competition includes the design, development, production, promotion, or sale of products or services competitive with those of the Company."

> "Employee agrees that, for a period of ____ years after termination of his/her employment, he/she will not compete, directly or indirectly, with the Company in any area of its business, if the duties of such competitive employment inherently require that Employee use or disclose any of the Company's Proprietary Information. Competition includes the design, development, production, promotion, or sale of products or services competitive with those of the Company."

The second clause, with the added proviso, is naturally much weaker in its restrictiveness. However, it may be enforceable in situations where the first is not, and may in any event act as an effective deterrent.

Consulting Option

> "Employee agrees that, upon termination of employment, other than termination by the Company, the Company shall have the option to retain Employee as a part-time consultant in any area in which he/she has served the Company, for a period of ___ to years, to be specified at the time of the Company's exercise of its option under this paragraph. During the period that Employee acts as such part-time consultant, he/she shall make his/her services available to the Company at mutually agreeable times and places and for at least ___ days per month. Employee shall be paid for such services at the rate of . . . per eight-hour day, or at such other rate as is mutually agreed. During the period that Employee acts as such part-time consultant, he/she shall not provide similar services to any other party without the prior written consent of the Company."

This sort of clause is often used in conjunction with the straight noncompetition clause, especially if the employee is particularly valuable, or if he/she worked for a competitor and could cause harm. If must be used carefully, however, since the agreement must call for enough work and a high enough rate of pay to be considered "real" by a judge. In fact, for the unique employee, you may be willing to include the following provision, as further assurances that a court will not find your noncompetition clause to be "unreasonable."

> "In the event that, solely as a result of Employee's noncompetition or consulting covenants contained in this agreement, Employee is unable, after diligent efforts, to secure suitable employment, considering his/her education, training, and abilities, then the Company shall, at its option, either have the option of (i) release Employee from such of his/her obiligations as will allow him/her to secure such employment, or (ii) pay to Employee, for the balance of the term of his/her noncompetition or consulting covenants, a periodic amount equal to the salary at termination. In the event that the option described in clause (ii) is exercised, Employee agrees to be available, during normal business hours on a full-time basis, for the performance of such assignments as the Company may direct."

Nonsolicitation Covenants

"Employee agrees that for a period of ___ years after termination of employment, he/she will not solicit or accept business, directly or indirectly, as to products or services competitive with those of the Company, from any of the Company's customers with whom he/she had contact within one year prior to his/her termination."

"Employee agrees that for a period of ___ years after termination of employment, he/she will not directly or indirectly induce or solicit any of the Company's employees to leave their employment, nor will he/she accept employment with any person who was employed by the Company during the year preceding Employee's termination; provided that such limitation on acceptance of employment shall only apply if Employee's salary at the time of his termination was at least $ ___ per year."

(The purpose of the last proviso is to limit the restriction "reasonably" to key employees.)

H
CONSULTANT CONFIDENTIAL PROVISIONS

> In connection with Consultant's work for the Company, Consultant may be given access to certain information which remains a trade secret of the Company. During that time, Consultant agrees not to use or disclose such information except as directed by an authorized representative of the Company.
>
> Consultant also agrees to disclose promptly in writing to the Company any inventions or useful ideas conceived or discovered in connection with his/her work for the Company.
>
> Consultant hereby assigns and agrees to assign at no additional consideration these inventions and ideas to the Company, and agrees to execute all papers the Company requests in order to establish and maintain the Company's interest in them. The expenses of obtaining patents on these inventions or ideas shall be paid by the Company.

As a practical matter, most experienced consultants will require you to define and describe your trade secrets in some detail. After all, consultants make their living by hopping from one firm to another in the same industry. They may justifiably insist on a strict limitation of their obligations not to use what you consider to be your trade secrets.

A word to consultants: don't sign these things if you can avoid it. Remember more than one person can possess the same trade secret, discovered independently. If you have to sign, insist on a precise definition.

I

CUSTOMER CONTACT SHEET

Name: ______________________________
Address: ______________________________
Phone: ______________________________

Date	Name	Dept./ Position	* Type Contact	Comments

* CT = call to
  CF = call from
  MT = meeting

Index